SHAKESPEARE'S PROVERB LORE

His Use of the *Sententiae* of
Leonard Culman and Publilius Syrus

Shakespeare's Proverb Lore

His Use of the *Sententiae* of
Leonard Culman and Publilius Syrus

CHARLES G. SMITH

HARVARD UNIVERSITY PRESS
Cambridge, Massachusetts

Distributed in Great Britain by
Oxford University Press, London

Library of Congress Catalog Card Number 63–17213

Printed in the United States of America

To the Memory of

My Father and My Mother

ROBERT DANIEL SMITH

and

JANETTE PASCHAL SMITH

PREFACE

This monograph is the by-product of a long and lively interest in the proverb lore of the English Renaissance, primarily with reference to Spenser. For the past six years the material presented here has been my chief interest. The main purpose of this adventurous enterprise is to exhibit proverb lore found in Shakespeare with striking parallels discovered in the *Sententiae Pueriles* of Leonard Culman and in the *Sententiae* of Publilius Syrus. It is a deliberately limited study; its subtitle furnishes a key to its chief concern and its limitation.

In his *Elizabethan Proverb Lore* and in his *Dictionary of the Proverbs in England*, Morris Palmer Tilley has given special prominence to Shakespeare because Shakespeare "knew the proverb more thoroughly than anyone else." Tilley's findings have been of invaluable help in the present investigation and I have made extensive use of his material. However, I have not always followed him, but nowhere have I called attention to the fact. The material which I have presented has, I hope, its own validity.

In order to make the proverbial material considered in this monograph readily accessible, I have supplied three indexes: a distribution index to the proverb lore quoted from Shakespeare; a Latin word index to all the *sententiae* quoted; and, a catchword index to the proverb lore quoted from Shakespeare and to the translations of all the *sententiae* quoted.

To colleagues and other friends I owe kindnesses far too many to enumerate. For many years I have studied proverbs under the influence of the three most outstanding American authorities on proverb lore: Archer Taylor, the late Morris Palmer Tilley, and Bartlett Jere Whiting. I am grateful to Professor Taylor and

Professor Whiting for their kindly interest, their critical reading of my manuscript, and their detailed suggestions for revision: to both of them I owe a special debt of thanks. To Dr. Roy F. Butler I owe particular and emphatic thanks for help in translating some of the *sententiae* and for provocative observations and judgments. I am under happy obligation to Mrs. J. Homer Caskey and Mrs. Arthur Smith for their critical reading of my manuscript and for their helpful suggestions.

I desire to express my appreciation to the officers and staff of the Baylor University Library for their cooperation and their assistance; to Miss Estaline Cox and Miss Lulu Stine I am especially grateful. To the University of Michigan Library I am indebted for the use of its copy of the *Sentences* of Publilius Syrus edited by Jules Chenu, printed in Paris in 1835. For practical encouragement in the form of leisure to complete this study, I am under obligation to Baylor University; for this encouragement I wish to thank Dr. E. Hudson Long, Chairman of the Department of English.

For valuable assistance in the preparation of this material for publication, including the making of the typescript, I am indebted to many of my students. To the following I owe a debt of gratitude: JoEllen Dahlor, Peggy Hightower, Vernita Holzschuh, Joyce Keele, Cynthia Kollhoff, Jane Mabray, Marilyn Marlow, Ersilee Ruth Parker, Ann Hope Perkison, Dell Bruner Rogers, Barbara Sexton, and Roberta Tharp.

My greatest debt is to my wife, Cornelia Marschall, who, several years ago, published an article on the use of proverbs ("Proverb Lore in *The Ring and the Book*," PMLA, LVI: March 1941, 219–229). To her, my steadfast comrade and good companion, I express my gratitude for her judicious criticism and her unfailing encouragement. I owe more to her mind and spirit than can be said.

CHARLES G. SMITH

Waco, Texas
September 9, 1962

CONTENTS

SHAKESPEARE'S PROVERB LORE

His Use of the *Sententiae* of
Leonard Culman and Publilius Syrus

INTRODUCTION

I

In the exploration of any aspect of Shakespeare's proverb lore it is important to remember not only that the Elizabethans loved proverbs but also that they were proverb conscious: they were steeped in proverbs. They knew that "when we deal with proverbs we are close to man and often near to wisdom."[1] We should not forget that their conception of what was proverbial was elastic. Today we scrutinize collections of proverbs and make distinctions between proverbs and *sententiae*, but in the English Renaissance proverbs and *sententiae* were considered essentially the same. In this study, therefore, no distinction is made between them: such a distinction rigidly enforced on the material presented here breaks down.

Thomas W. Baldwin,[2] Virgil K. Whitaker,[3] and many others have made fruitful investigations of Shakespeare's literary background, but there is much still to be done. In the present monograph the results of a thorough study of the possible influence of the *Sententiae Pueriles* of Leonard Culman[4] and the *Sententiae* of

[1] B. J. Whiting, Francis W. Bradley, Richard Jente, Archer Taylor, and M. P. Tilley, "The Study of Proverbs," *Modern Language Forum*, XXIV: 2 (June 1939), 83.
[2] *William Shakspere's Small Latine & Lesse Greeke*, 2 vols., Urbana, 1944.
[3] *Shakespeare's Use of Learning: An Inquiry into the Growth of his Mind & Art*, San Marino, California, 1953.
[4] Leonard Culman [Leonhardus Culmannus] was born at Crailsheim, Germany, on February 22, 1497 or 1498. His preuniversity schooling was in Halle, Dinkelsbühl, Nürnberg, and Saalfeld. He studied later at Erfurt and Leipzig. He served as a schoolmaster in Bamberg, Ansbach, and Nürnberg. Finally, he became an evangelical clergyman. In 1558 he took a pastorate in Bernstatt near the capital city of Ulm. In this region in 1562 he died. For further information concerning him consult *Allgemeine Deutsche Biographie*, Leipzig, 1876.

Publilius Syrus[5] on Shakespeare are presented. Although the main endeavor is to demonstrate the possible use Shakespeare may have made of the *sententiae* of Culman and Publilius Syrus, the evidence presented is not to be considered as an effort to establish sources.

In addition to the time spent in discovering in Culman and Publilius Syrus noteworthy parallels with sententious material in Shakespeare, much time has been spent searching out other striking parallels in Shakespeare's literary environment. When Shakespeare was in school, in all probability he, like every other Elizabethan schoolboy, was taught to keep a commonplace book of sayings drawn from his reading. Without question, he came under the influence of many classical writers. It is generally agreed that sometime during his life he read Cato, Cicero, Horace, Ovid, Plautus, Seneca, Terence, and Vergil. In this monograph, pertinent parallels found in these and other classical writers are presented. These parallels serve to indicate that, although Shakespeare may have been influenced by a maxim found in Culman or Publilius Syrus, he may have been influenced also by the same maxim, or some variation of the maxim, found in some other writer. Since many of the proverbs in Shakespeare considered in this investigation are widespread in both classical and Elizabethan literature, the probability is that in using most of these proverbs Shakespeare was influenced by more than one source and occasionally by a multiplicity of sources. Specific source ascription for proverb lore is usually unwarranted.

In this study when sententious material in Shakespeare is presented with parallels from Culman or Publilius Syrus only, it is because no other parallels have been discovered. An exhaustive search for classical parallels, however, has not been made, since

---

[5] Publilius Syrus belonged to the age of Julius Caesar. Of Syrian origin, he came to Rome probably from Antioch. For some time he was a slave in Rome. His talents and virtues gaining for him his freedom, he began to write plays called *mimes*. His great success attracted the attention of Julius Caesar, who called him to Rome and showered honors upon him. His plays have all been lost. Only his moral maxims—his pithy *sententiae*—have survived.

the supplying of such parallels is of secondary importance in the present endeavor. When in Culman or Publilius Syrus a parallel with sententious material in Shakespeare has been found, but no parallel can be found elsewhere in Elizabethan literature or in classical literature thought to have been available to Shakespeare, the probability that Shakespeare got it from Culman or Publilius Syrus is of course strengthened.

II

The influence of Leonard Culman's *Sententiae Pueriles* on Shakespeare has been singularly neglected. The *Sententiae Pueriles* is a collection of Latin maxims from divers authors which apparently every Elizabethan schoolboy was required to commit to memory. J. Q. Adams suggests that Shakespeare committed it to "the ventricle of memory"[6] and says:

> There is nothing unlikely about the assertion that Shakespeare secured a country school, probably not far from Stratford, and that for a few years he taught Lilly's *Grammatica Latina*, the *Sententiae Pueriles*, Ovid, Terence, Plautus, and such other books as he had studied under his Stratford schoolmasters.[7]

There is some evidence that Culman's *Sententiae Pueriles* was well known to Shakespeare's contemporaries. In 1569–1570 it was entered on the Stationer's Register. Baldwin has given a good account of the use of the little book in Elizabethan England. He says that it "was very widely used in Shakspere's time," and that "he may very well have memorized the collection."[8] Whitaker asserts that "Shakespeare almost certainly used" it, since it was "a universal textbook."[9] The *sententiae* in the collection are arranged alphabetically in groups of maxims of two words, maxims of three words, and so on. Culman compiled the collection

---

[6] *Love's Labor's Lost*, IV, ii, 70–71.
[7] *Life of William Shakespeare*, Boston, 1923, p. 92; cf. pp. 55–56; 90–93.
[8] *William Shakspere's Small Latine & Lesse Greeke*, I, 593; cf. pp. 591–595.
[9] *Shakespeare's Use of Learning*, p. 21.

probably not long before 1540. Evidently he collected his maxims from numerous sources. Undoubtedly he got many of them from Erasmus, several from Cato, and a few from Seneca. A copy of Culman's book printed at Nürnberg in 1540 is in the Library of the University of Illinois; a copy printed at Leipzig in 1544 is in the British Museum.[10] In the present investigation the edition printed in London in 1658 with a translation by Charles Hoole is used.[11] In the 1658 edition there are 1173 *sententiae*.[12]

Edmund Malone (1741–1812) was perhaps the first to suggest that Shakespeare was acquainted with the collection.[13] In 1887 James Orchard Halliwell-Phillipps, after examining the book, asserted that Shakespeare probably studied and used it. He says:

> The Sententiae Pueriles was, in all probability, the little manual by the aid of which he first learned to construe Latin, for in one place, at least, he all but literally translates a brief passage, and there are in his plays several adaptations of its sentiments. It was then sold for a penny, equivalent to about our present shilling, and contains a large collection of brief sentences collected from a variety of authors, with a distinct selection of moral and religious paragraphs, the latter intended for the use of boys on Saints' Days.[14]

[10] Cf. Baldwin, I, 592. There is a copy of the edition printed in Boston in 1723 in the Library of Congress and a copy of the same edition in the Huntington Library. A copy of the 1639 edition is in the Folger Shakespeare Library; a copy of the 1658 edition is in the British Museum.

[11] The 1658 edition has been carefully compared with the edition printed in London in 1639 and the edition printed in Boston in 1723. On the basis of these comparisons a few minor emendations have been made in the *sententiae* cited from the 1658 edition. Hoole's translation has not been consistently used, and some of his spelling has been modernized. All old type-forms have been modernized in accordance with modern usage.

[12] The 1540 edition, perhaps the first, contains a few more *sententiae* than the 1658 edition: there are a few *sententiae* in the 1540 edition that are not in the 1658 edition, and vice versa. The 1639 edition, the 1658 edition, and the 1723 edition all contain the same 1173 *sententiae*. In ascertaining the number of *sententiae* in each of these three editions, the section appended at the end of each edition on "The more common and ordinary rules for children's behaviour" has been left out of account.

[13] *Variorum* (1821), II, 104; cf. Baldwin, I, 591.

[14] *Outlines* (1887), I, 53; cf. Baldwin, I, 591.

Apparently H. R. D. Anders, in 1904, was the first to point out definite passages in Shakespeare that have parallels in Culman. He says:

> I cannot say exactly what the 'brief passage' is, which Halliwell-Phillipps refers to. The following are some sentences which have a resemblance to passages in Shakespeare. But they are so general in character, that we can scarcely infer anything definite from them.
>
> *Belli exitus incertus.* Compare Coriol., V, iii, 140:
>
> > "Thou know'st, great son,
> > The end of war's uncertain."
>
> *Doloris medicus tempus.* Comp. Gent. of Ver., III, ii, 15: "A little time, my lord, will kill that grief." Comp. too, Act III, i, 243; and Cymbeline III, v, 37: "The cure whereof, my lord, 'Tis time must do."
>
> *Varia et mutabilis semper foemina.* Compare 1 Henry IV., Act. II, iii, 111: "constant you are, But yet a woman."
>
> *Somnus mortis imago.* Compare Cymb., II, ii, 31: "O sleep, thou ape of death;" or Macbeth, II, iii, 81: "sleep, death's counterfeit."[15]

The second investigator to point out parallel passages in Shakespeare and in Culman was Morris Palmer Tilley: in 1926 he cited six hitherto unnoted parallels.[16] In 1944 Baldwin cited two additional new parallels;[17] in 1950 Tilley cited one more previously unnoted parallel.[18] Before this investigation was undertaken, apparently no other parallels had been cited.

In the present monograph the thirteen parallels discovered by Anders, Tilley, and Baldwin, augmented by supplementary Culman and Shakespeare parallels and supported by selected

---

[15] *Shakespeare's Books*, Berlin, 1904, pp. 47-48.
[16] *Elizabethan Proverb Lore*, New York, 1926, "List of Proverbs," nos. 111, 258, 398, 642, 732, 753.
[17] *William Shakspere's Small Latine & Lesse Greeke*, I, 592.
[18] *Proverbs in England*, Ann Arbor, 1950, N307.

parallels from Shakespeare's classical background, are presented in the "List of Proverbs" in the following entries: 32, 49, 64, 130, 133, 182, 219, 232, 271, 296, 301, 321, 337. In addition to these previously discovered parallels, 196 hitherto unnoted parallels are pointed out. Of these 209 different proverbs in Shakespeare, 160 have one Culman parallel; 35 have two; 11 have three; 2 have four; and 1 has five. In one instance there are two Culman parallels that have the same wording.[19] The 196 hitherto unnoted parallels, in conjunction with the 13 previously discovered, give strong support to the suggestion made by Adams and Baldwin that Shakespeare memorized Culman's little book. Many of these parallels are striking; many of them throw new light on Shakespeare's use of proverbs.

III

Some explanation of the editions of Publilius Syrus used in the present investigation is in order. The earliest collection of the *sententiae* of Publilius Syrus, compiled perhaps sometime during the first century A.D., was possibly entirely Publilian. Since that time, however, many *sententiae* taken from other writers, Seneca for example, have been foisted into the original collection. It is regrettably true that

the sententious verses which passed under the name of Publilius Syrus during the Middle Ages and Renaissance and even later are troublesome to find. We have had many editions since Erasmus's text published with the *Disticha Catonis* in 1514 and . . . the complications of separating the genuine and spurious parts we . . . need not attempt.[20]

---

[19] Cf. "List of Proverbs," no. 183. In no. 197 there are two Culman parallels that have essentially the same wording.

[20] Whiting, Bradley, Jente, Taylor, Tilley, pp. 58–59. For a comprehensive study of the various editions of Publilius Syrus consult the Introduction to R. A. H. Bickford-Smith's 1895 edition.

Apparently every medieval and Renaissance schoolboy studied Publilius Syrus. Professor John Matthews Manly, evidently confusing the *Sententiae Pueriles* of Leonard Culman with the *Sententiae* of Publilius Syrus, says that "one of the first books in the course in Latin was the *Sententiae Pueriles* of Publilius Sirus," and suggests that it "was familiar to every mediaeval schoolboy."[21]

The two collections of Publilius Syrus used in the present study[22] are comprehensive. They contain about 900 *sententiae* not in Erasmus's school collection. Of the 270 *sententiae* attributed to Publilius Syrus by Erasmus, 266 are in one of the two collections used in this study. In many of the *sententiae*, however, there are slight variations in the wording and in the spelling. Erasmus's school collection was accessible to Shakespeare, and it is altogether possible that he may have come in contact with many of the other *sententiae* in the two collections used in the present study: for example, he may have come in contact with them in one of the several collections of *sententiae* published either before or during the Elizabethan period. Shakespeare did not stop reading when he left school. Hence, striking parallels in Shakespeare with the *sententiae* in the two collections used in this study have been diligently sought out.

The fact that many of the parallels of Publilius Syrus exhibited in the present monograph are not in Erasmus's school collection does not prevent their having significance: some of them are illuminating. For example, the *sententia* of Publilius Syrus exhibited in entry no. 62 in the "List of Proverbs," although it is not in the school collection, gives every evidence of being highly significant. Hitherto no one has found a satisfactory source or springboard for Ulysses' famous speech on degree in *Troilus and Cressida*. The *sententia* presented in entry no. 62 expresses the leading idea of Ulysses' speech patently. It is quite possible that Shakespeare,

[21] *Chaucer's "Canterbury Tales,"* New York, 1928, p. 549.
[22] *Sentences* of Publilius Syrus edited by Jules Chenu, 1835, and *Sententiae* of Publilius Syrus edited by J. Wight Duff and Arnold M. Duff, 1934; cf. "Books Frequently Cited."

employing the devices of amplification (with which he was thoroughly familiar) and giving his imagination full reign, in Ulysses' speech used this *sententia* to create one of his finest compositions.

In his *Elizabethan Proverb Lore* Tilley has identified no less than twenty-eight parallels in Publilius Syrus with sententious material in Shakespeare.[23] It is incredible that previous to Tilley only three parallels had been pointed out: one by Isaac Reed (1742–1807) and two by Edmund Malone.[24] Only one of these is included in Tilley's findings.[25]

In discussing the influence of Publilius Syrus on Shakespeare, Baldwin considers only four parallels. Apparently he thinks only one of Tilley's parallels is significant. He says, "Professor Tilley notes several other parallels with Shakspere;" but, since "these were not in the school collection" prepared by Erasmus, he disregards them.[26] However, three other parallels pointed out by Tilley, but overlooked by Baldwin, are in Erasmus's collection.[27] A copy of that collection, published in London in 1572, is in the British Museum. The findings presented here are based on that copy. In the present investigation—in addition to the seven parallels pointed out by Reed, Malone, and Tilley—forty-six

[23] Tilley used the 1835 edition of Publilius Syrus edited by Jules Chenu, one of the two editions used in the present investigation. His twenty-eight parallels are to be found in his "List of Proverbs" in the following entries: 7, 52, 69, 110, 143, 144, 200, 209, 211, 258, 278, 318, 322, 360, 377, 446, 515, 516, 623, 633, 651, 659, 661, 686, 692, 701, 738. These parallels are presented in the "List of Proverbs" in the present study in the following entries: 7, 16, 30, 55, 64, 75, 92, 95, 129, 132, 146, 147, 169, 190, 203, 220, 248, 249, 254, 255, 256, 257, 273, 294, 306, 317, 328, 336.

[24] Cf. *Variorum* (1821), VI, 401; VIII, 332; XX, 110; Baldwin, I, 603–604. The parallel pointed out by Reed is included in the "List of Proverbs" in this study, no. 117; the two by Malone in nos. 190, 201.

[25] Cf. Tilley, *Elizabethan Proverb Lore*, "List of Proverbs," no. 692. Tilley's finding is reported in the "List of Proverbs" in this study, no. 190.

[26] *William Shakspere's Small Latine & Lesse Greeke*, I, 595–596, 604. The parallel pointed out by Tilley which Baldwin considers is to be found in Tilley's *Elizabethan Proverb Lore*, "List of Proverbs," no. 701; cf. the "List of Proverbs" in this study, no. 336.

[27] Cf. Tilley, *Elizabethan Proverb Lore*, "List of Proverbs," nos. 110, 738. These are presented in the "List of Proverbs" in this study, nos. 132, 256, 257.

hitherto unnoted parallels in Erasmus's collection have been adduced.[28] Besides these 53 parallels, in this study 127 additional parallels, not in the school collection, are presented. Of these 127 parallels, 23 were cited first by Tilley;[29] the remaining 104 have been cited for the first time in this study.

A total of 180 parallels in Shakespeare (many of them occurring several times) with *sententiae* of Publilius Syrus have now been discovered and are exhibited in this monograph. Of these 180 different proverbs, 147 have one Publilius Syrus parallel; 30 have two; 2 have three; and 1 has five. On the basis of only four parallels, Baldwin concludes that "some of Shakspere's sentential wisdom thus derives ultimately from Publius Syrus."[30] The material presented in this study impressively reinforces Baldwin's statement: supported by 53 parallels in the school collection and 127 parallels not in the school collection, one is amply warranted in suggesting that some of Shakespeare's proverbial wisdom "derives ultimately" from Publilius Syrus. It should be noted that 34 of these 127 bastard *sententiae* of Publilius Syrus are supported by parallels in Culman.[31] Since Shakespeare probably

---

[28] These 53 parallels are presented in the "List of Proverbs" in the present study and are marked with an asterisk. They are to be found in the following entries: 4, 7, 13, 29, 41, 44, 50, 51, 53, 67, 88, 94, 105, 106, 116, 117, 122, 132, 134, 145, 152, 154, 161, 172, 184, 188, 190, 199, 201, 215, 216, 222, 226, 227, 244, 245, 250, 256, 257, 259, 264, 272, 275, 291, 299, 310, 314, 322, 324, 334, 336, 338, 345. No. 94 includes two of Publilius Syrus's *sententiae* found in Erasmus's collection. The 1572 edition of Erasmus's *Catonis Disticha* includes his collection of the *sententiae* of Publilius Syrus; cf. Baldwin, I, 595.

[29] Cf. *Elizabethan Proverb Lore*, "List of Proverbs," nos. 7, 52, 69, 143, 144, 200, 209, 211, 258, 278, 318, 322, 360, 377, 446, 515, 516, 623, 633, 651, 659, 661, 686. These are presented in the "List of Proverbs" in this study in the following entries: 7, 16, 30, 55, 64, 75, 92, 95, 129, 146, 147, 169, 203, 220, 248, 249, 254, 255, 273, 294, 306, 317, 328.

[30] *William Shakspere's Small Latine & Lesse Greeke*, I, 604.

[31] These *sententiae* of Publilius Syrus, supported by parallels in Culman from whom Shakespeare may have taken them, are to be found in the "List of Proverbs" in this study in the following entries: 2, 16, 30, 47, 54, 55, 64, 90, 97, 120, 121, 124, 128, 148, 149, 157, 180, 182, 183, 186, 206, 214, 219, 230, 241, 246, 265, 267, 276, 306, 315, 323, 326.

read Seneca, who appropriated many of the *sententiae* of Publilius Syrus, it is possible that Shakespeare got some of Publilius Syrus's maxims from Seneca.[32]

IV

Of the 346 different proverbs in Shakespeare considered in the present study, 166 have Culman parallels but no Publilius Syrus parallels; 137 have Publilius Syrus parallels but no Culman parallels; 43 have both Culman and Publilius Syrus parallels. It is possible that Shakespeare got some of these proverbs directly or indirectly from Erasmus: 82 have parallels in the *Adagia*; 8 have parallels in Erasmus's other works. Since many of these proverbs were widespread in Elizabethan literature, Shakespeare probably got some of them from his contemporaries.

The twenty-five parallels with Shakespeare found in Cato, never before pointed out, should not be overlooked.[33] (Prior to the present investigation, apparently only one parallel had been noted.)[34] Some of these parallels are striking. For example, if Shakespeare did not get "Learn of the wise" (*As You Like It*, III, ii, 69) from Culman, he probably got it from Cato's *Disticha*, iv, 23: *Disce sed a doctis.*[35]

It is noteworthy that of the 346 different proverbs in Shakespeare considered in this study at least 162 have here, for the first time,

---

[32] In the "List of Proverbs" in this study parallels from both Seneca and Publilius Syrus are to be found in the following entries: 29, 30, 47, 53, 54, 64, 67, 84, 90, 105, 116, 117, 120, 125, 132, 144, 178, 182, 189, 210, 214, 225, 236, 249, 262, 281, 289, 306, 315, 324, 343, 345. Note especially the parallels in entry nos. 84, 105, 178, 182, 189, 225, 262, 345.

[33] These parallels are cited in the "List of Proverbs" in this study in the following entries: 10, 28, 30, 52, 53, 61, 68, 97, 112, 156, 171, 176, 187, 207, 214, 221, 230, 243, 258, 267, 271, 290, 304, 319, 338.

[34] Cf. Baldwin, I, 603. Baldwin says: "Curiously enough, only one parallel, so far as I have observed, has been noted with Cato proper." The parallel he cites is not relevant to the present investigation.

[35] Cf. "List of Proverbs" in this study, no. 171.

been authenticated.[36] Of these 162 proverbs, 70 have Culman parallels but no Publilius Syrus parallels; 67 have Publilius Syrus parallels but no Culman parallels; 25 have both Culman and Publilius Syrus parallels. The fact that only a few of these proverbs were current in Elizabethan literature increases the probability of their having been taken from Culman or Publilius Syrus. In some instances, when one of these proverbs does occur elsewhere in Elizabethan literature, it is possible that each writer who uses it got it directly from Culman or Publilius Syrus.[37]

The multiplicity of the parallels in the *sententiae* of Culman and Publilius Syrus with proverb lore in Shakespeare adduced in this study is impressive. A careful examination of these parallels impels one to believe that Shakespeare wrote under the influence of the *sententiae* of Culman and Publilius Syrus and that he used many of those *sententiae*.[38] Shakespeare does not merely put them into English dress: he plunges them into the solvent of his imagination, and, in absorbing them with poetic freshness into the fabric of his material, he takes the stiffness and rigidity out of them. He has so transmuted many of them that they are difficult to recognize; and, unless one has a close acquaintance with them, one's ears are likely to be deaf to their presence and their value. Often Shakespeare merely alludes to a proverb obliquely; if we are acquainted with the proverb, the passage takes on meaning; if we are not, we miss some of the overtones of the passage.

[36] To determine whether the material from Shakespeare in the "List of Proverbs" in this study has been previously established as proverbial, consult the references cited at the end of each entry. In the entries where no references are given no authentication of the material has been found. In the following entries, although references are cited, the material from Shakespeare has not hitherto been authenticated as proverbial: 8, 23, 57, 82, 90, 103, 111, 121, 124, 125, 126, 127, 129, 134, 136, 141, 142, 178, 183, 193, 203, 207, 208, 209, 213, 214, 240, 253, 255, 264, 267, 268, 299, 300, 308, 310, 339, 341.

[37] Cf. "List of Proverbs," nos. 93, 151, 222, 344.

[38] The fact that Shakespeare employs many proverbs several times suggests that he had them stored up in his memory, unless, like Hamlet, he used his "tables" to record remarkable sayings. In *The Dark Lady of the Sonnets* Bernard Shaw represents Shakespeare as often crying out: "My tables! Meet it is I set it down" (*Hamlet*, I, v, 107).

It remains only to add a few observations concerning the significance of the sententious material presented in this monograph.

1. No material from Shakespeare has been included without careful consideration of its validity and its significance. Some of the identifications, however, probably will not go unchallenged.

2. Today some of the proverbs presented in this monograph are considered copybook platitudes and a few of them are thought of as mere trifles, but as employed by Shakespeare they are not without significance.

3. Although many of Shakespeare's proverbs were widespread in English literature during his lifetime, many of them are classical in their provenience.

4. The material presented in this study is further evidence of the soundness of the thesis that Shakespeare had a comprehensive knowledge of classical proverbs.

5. Much of the sententious material in Shakespeare that has never been authenticated as proverbial is undoubtedly the product of his creative imagination. From his study of *sententiae* in school he knew their telling power: he learned to think sententiously. It is to be hoped, however, that other researchers will find in the *sententiae* of Culman and Publilius Syrus, in other collections of *sententiae* in Shakespeare's literary environment, and in the Latin and Greek authors thought to have been accessible to him, undiscovered parallels for more of his proverb lore.

6. Unlike some of his contemporaries who seem to have employed proverbs largely as an ornamental device—Lyly for example—Shakespeare used proverb lore as a component in almost everything he wrote. This study of only one small part of his use of proverbs demonstrates that proverbial wisdom is vital in his thought and is, therefore, a deeply diffused humanism.

LIST OF PROVERBS

LIST OF PROVERBS

This is a list of Shakespeare's proverbs for which parallels in Leonard
Culman and Publilius Syrus have been discovered. The arrangement of
the proverbs with the parallel *sententiae* under each numbered boldface
heading, alphabetized according to a more or less arbitrarily selected
catchword, is as follows: 1. The proverbial material from Shakespeare,
taken from his *Complete Works* edited by George Lyman Kittredge and
arranged chronologically according to Kittredge's dating of the plays
and the poems. 2. Parallels from Leonard Culman's *Sententiae Pueriles*
and Publilius Syrus's *Sententiae*. The 1658 edition of Culman is used;
two collections of Publilius Syrus are used: the collection edited by
Jules Chenu, 1835, and the collection edited by J. Wight Duff and
Arnold M. Duff, 1934. The *sententiae* of Publilius Syrus marked by an
asterisk were in the Elizabethan school collection included in *Catonis
Disticha* prepared by Erasmus. 3. Parallels chiefly from Greek and
Latin authors and Erasmus: *Adagia*. (Nearly all of the sententious
material cited from Latin and Greek authors is taken from the Loeb
Classical Library editions. Many parallels also are cited from early or
contemporary English literature.) 4. References, primarily to modern
collections of proverbs.

Jul. Caesar, I, ii, 140–141: The fault, dear Brutus, is not in our stars,
But in ourselves, that we are underlings. ¶*All's Well*, I, i, 231–232:
Our remedies oft in ourselves do lie, Which we ascribe to heaven.
¶*K. Lear*, I, ii, 128–132: This is the excellent foppery of the world,
that, when we are sick in fortune, often the surfeit of our own behaviour,
we make guilty of our disasters the sun, the moon, and the stars; as if
we were villains on necessity.

Publilius Syrus (1934), 667: Stultum est queri de adversis, ubi culpa
est tua (Silly to grumble about misfortune when the fault's your own).

Homer, *Odyssey*, i, 32: Ὦ πόποι, οἷον δή νυ θεοὺς βροτοὶ αἰτιόωνται (Look you now, how ready mortals are to blame the gods). ¶ Aristotle, *N. Ethics*, iii, 1, 11: τῶν μὲν καλῶν ἑαυτόν, τῶν δ' αἰσχρῶν τὰ ἡδέα (It is absurd to blame external things, instead of blaming ourselves). ¶ Quintilian, *Inst. Orat.*, vi, Pref., 13: Frustra mala omnia ad crimen fortunae relegamus (It is in vain that we impute all our ills to fortune). ¶ Sidney, *Arcadia*, *Works* (Feuillerat), I, 156: You blame your fortune very wrongfully, since the fault is not in Fortune, but in you that cannot frame your selfe to your fortune.

2 A FRIEND IS KNOWN IN **ADVERSITY**

Pass. Pilgr., 20, 51–52: He that is thy friend indeed, He will help thee in thy need. ¶ *Hamlet*, III, ii, 218–219: Who in want a hollow friend doth try, Directly seasons him his enemy.

Culman, 10: Amicos inter adversa cognoscimus (We know our friends in adversity). ¶ *Ibid.*, 13: In adversis amicus probatur (A friend is tried in adversity). ¶ *Ibid.*, 16: Tempore adversitatis probatur amicus (A friend is tried in time of adversity). ¶ *Ibid.*, 17: Amici in rebus adversis cognoscuntur (Friends are known in adversity). ¶ *Ibid.*, 21: In adversis rebus amicus cognoscitur (A friend is known in adversity). ¶ Publilius Syrus (1934), 41: Amicum an nomen habeas aperit calamitas (Misfortune reveals whether you have a friend or only one in name).

Plautus, *Epidicus*, 113: Is est amicus, qui in re dubia re iuvat, ubi rest opus (A real friend in a pinch is a friend in deed, when deeds are needed). ¶ Erasmus, *Adagia*, 1055A: Amicus certus in re incerta cernitur (When fortune is fickle the faithful friend is found).

Cf. Tilley, *Prov. in Eng.*, F693, T301.

3 IN **ADVERSITY** A VALIANT MAN SUFFERS WISELY

Cf. no. 4: The virtue of adversity is patience

3 Hen. VI, III, i, 24–25: Embrace . . . sour adversity, For wise men say it is the wisest course. ¶ *Timon*, III, v, 31–32: He's truly valiant that can wisely suffer The worst that man can breathe.

Culman, 19: Fortis animi est, non perturbari in rebus adversis (It is the part of a valiant man not to be troubled in adversity).

4   THE VIRTUE OF ADVERSITY IS PATIENCE

Cf. no. 3: In adversity a valiant man suffers wisely

Com. of Errors, IV, iv, 20–21: 'Tis for me to be patient! I am in adversity. ¶*Othello*, I, iii, 206–207: What cannot be preserv'd when fortune takes, Patience her injury a mock'ry makes. ¶*Two Noble K.*, II, i, 27–28: They have patience to make any adversity asham'd.

Culman, 17: Adversa aequo animo sunt toleranda (Adversities are to be undergone with a patient mind). ¶*Publilius Syrus (1934), 111: Cuivis dolori remedium est patientia (Endurance is the cure for any pain). ¶*Ibid.* (1835), 229: Et miseriarum portus est patientia (Patience is affliction's haven).

5 AFFLICTIONS ARE SENT US BY GOD FOR OUR GOOD

Cf. no. 233: Bitter pills may have wholesome effects

Cymb., III, ii, 33: Some griefs are med'cinable. ¶*Winter's T.*, II, i, 121–122: This action I now go on [imprisonment] Is for my better grace.

Culman, 28: Adversitates nostrae a Deo (Our crosses are from God).

Seneca, *De Prov.*, iii, 2: Quaedam incommoda pro is esse quibus accidunt (Ills are sometimes for the good of those to whom they come).

Cf. Tilley, *Prov. in Eng.*, A53.

6   WE ARE MADE WISER BY AGE

Lucrece, 1550: Priam, why art thou old, and yet not wise? ¶*K. Lear*, I, iv, 261: As you are old and reverend, you should be wise. ¶*Ibid.*, v, 47–48: Thou shouldst not have been old till thou hadst been wise.

Culman, 5: Aetate prudentiores reddimur (We are made wiser by age). ¶*Ibid.*, 10: Ante annos prudentia nulla (There is no discretion before years). ¶*Ibid.*, 15: Praestantiores sunt senum sententiae (Old men's opinions are the best).

Euripides, *Phoenissae*, 529–530: ἐμπειρία ἔχει τι λέξαι τῶν νέων σοφώτερον (Experience can plead more wisely than the lips of youth).

¶Terence, *Adelphoe*, 832: Aetate sapimus rectius (We get wiser as we grow older). ¶Cicero, *De Sen.*, xix, 67: Mens enim et ratio et consilium in senibus est (It is in old men that reason and good judgment are found). ¶Lucian, *Heracles*, 4: τὸ δὲ γῆρας ἔχει τι λέξαι τῶν νέων σοφώτερον (Old age has wiser words to say than youth). ¶Erasmus, *Adagia*, 929D: Aetate prudentiores reddimur (We are made wiser by age).

7 WHAT CANNOT BE **ALTERED** MUST BE BORNE, NOT BLAMED (LAMENTED)

Cf. no. 47: What cannot be cured must be endured; no. 105: It is folly to fear what cannot be avoided

Two Gent., III, i, 241: Cease to lament for that thou canst not help.
¶*Coriol.*, IV, vii, 11–12: I must excuse What cannot be amended.

* Publilius Syrus (1934), 206: Feras non culpes quod mutari non potest (What can't be changed you should bear, not blame).

Erasmus, *Adagia*, 117D: Feras non culpes, quod vitari non potest (What can't be avoided you should bear, not blame).

Cf. Tilley, *Eliz. Prov. Lore*, 52, *Prov. in Eng.*, A231.

8 **ANGER** PUNISHES ITSELF

Cymb., I, i, 134–135: Harm not yourself with your vexation. I am senseless of your wrath.

Culman, 6: Ira tormentum sui ipsius (Anger is the torment of itself).
¶Publilius Syrus (1835), 1025: Expetit poenas iratus ab alio; a se ipso exigit (Anger would inflict punishment on another; meanwhile, it tortures itself).

Erasmus, *Similia*, 588C: Iracundia sibi nocet saepenumero, cum aliis nocere studet (Anger often injures itself, when it strives to injure others).

Cf. Tilley, *Prov. in Eng.*, A247.

9 HE INVITES DANGER WHO INDULGES IN **ANGER**

Cf. no. 219: Nothing is well said or done in anger

Ant. & Cleop., IV, i, 9–10: Never anger Made good guard for itself. Publilius Syrus (1835), 684: Petit, qui irascitur, periculum sibi (He invites danger who indulges in anger).

10   MODERATE YOUR **ANGER**

All's Well, II, iii, 222: Do not plunge thyself too far in anger.
Culman, 2: Iracundiam tempera (Moderate thy passion). ¶ *Ibid.*, 24: Ponere modum irae & voluptati, bonum est (It is good to keep a measure in anger and pleasure).
Cato, *Collectio Dis. Vulg.*, 45: Iracundiam rege (Control your anger).

11 A MAN IS THE **ARCHITECT** OF HIS OWN FORTUNE

Lucrece, 1069: I am the mistress of my fate. ¶ *Jul. Caesar*, I, ii, 139: Men at some time are masters of their fates. ¶ *Othello*, I, iii, 322–323: 'Tis in ourselves that we are thus or thus.
Publilius Syrus (1835), 286: Fortunam cuique mores confingunt sui (His own character is the arbiter of everyone's fortune).
Plautus, *Trinummus*, 363: Nam sapiens quidem pol ipsus fingit fortunam sibi (For I tell you, a man, a wise man, molds his own destiny). ¶ Sallust, *Ad Caesarem De Rep.*, i, 2: In carminibus Appius ait, fabrum esse suae quemque fortunae (Appius says in his verses that every man is the architect of his own fortune). ¶ Erasmus, *Adagia*, 532E: Sui cuique mores fingunt fortunam (His own character shapes each man's fortune).
Cf. Taverner, 35; Bacon, *Promus*, 357; Tilley, *Prov. in Eng.*, M126.

12 AN **ASS** THOUGH LADEN WITH GOLD STILL EATS THISTLES

Jul. Caesar, IV, i, 21–27: He shall but bear them as the ass bears gold, To groan and sweat under the business ... Then take we down his

load, and turn him off (Like to the empty ass) to shake his ears And graze in commons.
Culman, 17: Asinus mavult stramina, quam aurum (An ass had rather have straw than gold).
Cf. Tilley, *Prov. in Eng.*, A360.

13 DISPOSITIONS NATURALLY BAD NEED NO TEACHER

2 Hen. VI, V, i, 191: A subtle traitor needs no sophister.
*Publilius Syrus (1934), 369: Malae naturae numquam doctore indigent (Bad natures never lack an instructor).

14   TO BE RATHER THAN TO SEEM

Lucrece, 600: Thou art not what thou seem'st. ¶*1 Hen. IV*, V, iv, 140: Thou art not what thou seem'st. ¶*Meas. for Meas.*, III, ii, 40–41: That we were all, as some would seem to be, Free from our faults, as from faults seeming free! ¶*Othello*, III, iii, 126–128: Men should be what they seem; Or those that be not, would they might seem none! — Certain, men should be what they seem. ¶*Coriol.*, III, i, 218: Be that you seem. ¶*Ibid.*, ii, 46–47: To seem The same you are.

Publilius Syrus (1835), 800: Quid ipse sis, non quid habearis, interest (It matters not what you are thought to be, but what you are).
Aeschylus, *Seven agst. Thebes*, 592: οὐ γὰρ δοκεῖν ἄριστος, ἀλλ' εἶναι θέλει (His resolve is not to seem the bravest, but to be). ¶Cicero, *De Offic.*, ii, 12, 43: Praeclare Socrates hanc viam ad gloriam proximam et quasi compendiariam dicebat esse, si quis id ageret, ut, qualis haberi vellet, talis esset (Socrates used to express it so admirably: "The nearest way to glory—a short cut, as it were—is to strive to be what you wish to be thought to be"). ¶Sallust, *Catilina*, liv, 6: Esse quam videri bonus malebat (He preferred to be, rather than to seem, virtuous). ¶Ovid, *Tristia*, v, 13, 26: Quod non es, ne videare, cave (Beware of seeming what you are not). ¶Erasmus, *Adagia*, 990A: Cura esse, quod audis (Take care to be what you are reported to be).
Cf. Bacon, *Promus*, 509; Tilley, *Prov. in Eng.*, S214.

15   BECAUSE IS A WOMAN'S REASON

Two Gent., I, ii, 22–24: Your reason? —I have no other but a woman's reason: I think him so because I think him so. ¶ *Troilus & Cres.*, I, i, 108–109: Wherefore not afield? —Because not there. This woman's answer sorts.

Culman, 22: Nihil, praeter quod gliscit, novit foemina (A woman knoweth nothing but what she hath a mind to).

Cf. Tilley, *Prov. in Eng.*, B179.

16 BEWARE OF HIM WHO HAS ONCE DECEIVED YOU

Titus Andr., I, i, 301: I'll trust by leisure him that mocks me once. ¶ *3 Hen. VI*, IV, iv, 30: Trust not him that hath once broken faith. ¶ *2 Hen. IV*, III, i, 88–90: King Richard might create a perfect guess That great Northumberland, then false to him, Would of that seed grow to a greater falseness. ¶ *Othello*, I, iii, 293–294: Look to her, Moor, if thou hast eyes to see. She has deceiv'd her father, and may thee.

Culman, 18: Cavendum ab eo qui semel imposuit (We must beware of him that hath once deceived us). ¶ Publilius Syrus (1835), 136: Cave illum semper, qui tibi imposuit semel (Beware of him who has once deceived you).

Erasmus, *Adagia*, 915C: Cavendum ab eo, qui semel imposuit (We must beware of him who has once deceived us). ¶ Udall, *Apoph. of Erasm.*, 327:7: To mistrust an vntrustie persone is a poinct of wisedom.

Cf. Tilley, *Eliz. Prov. Lore*, 144, *Prov. in Eng.*, D180.

17   BLUSHING IS A TOKEN OF VIRTUE

Two Gent., V, iv, 165: I think the boy hath grace in him; he blushes. ¶ *2 Hen. IV*, II, ii, 80–83: Come, you virtuous ass, you bashful fool, must you be blushing? . . . What a maidenly man-at-arms are you become! ¶ *Much Ado*, IV, i, 35–39: Behold how like a maid she blushes here! . . . Comes not that blood as modest evidence To witness simple virtue?

Culman, 15: Rubor virtutis est color (Blushing is the colour of vertue).

Diogenes Laertius, *Diogenes*, vi, 54: ἰδών ποτε μειράκιον ἐρυθριῶν, "θάρρει," ἔφη· "τοιοῦτόν ἐστι τῆς ἀρετῆς τὸ χρῶμα" (One day he detected a youth blushing. "Courage," quoth he, "that is the hue of virtue").

Cf. Udall, *Apoph. of Erasm.*, 140:133; Tilley, *Prov. in Eng.*, B480.

18   WE ARE NOT BORN FOR OURSELVES ALONE

Timon, I, ii, 105: We are born to do benefits.

Culman, 7: Nemo sibi nascitur (Nobody is born for himself). ¶ *Ibid.*, 34: Nemo sibi soli natus est (No man is born for himself alone).

Cicero, *De Fin.*, ii, 14, 45: Non sibi se soli natum meminerit sed patriae, sed suis (Man was not born for self alone, but for country and for kindred). ¶ *Ibid.*, *De Offic.*, i, 7, 22: Non nobis solum nati sumus (We are not born for ourselves alone). ¶ Erasmus, *Adagia*, 1094E: Nemo sibi nascitur (No one is born for himself).

Cf. Tilley, *Prov. in Eng.*, B141.

19   EVERYONE AS HIS BUSINESS LIES

Cf. no. 320: Everyone should labor in his own vocation

1 Hen. IV, II, ii, 81: Every man to his business. ¶ *Hamlet*, I, v, 128–131: I hold it fit that we shake hands and part; You, as your business and desire shall point you, For every man hath business and desire, Such as it is.

Culman, 36: Vocatio cuique sua curanda (Everyone must look to his own calling).

Cf. Tilley, *Prov. in Eng.*, M104.

20   CALAMITY (EXTREMITY) STIRS UP THE WIT

Cf. no. 284: The things which hurt us teach us

Coriol., IV, i, 3–5: You were us'd To say extremity was the trier of spirits; That common chances common men could bear. ¶ *Two Noble K.*, I, i, 118: Extremity . . . sharpens sundry wits.

Culman, 10: Adversa saepe excitant ingenium (Crosses do ofttimes stir up the wit). ¶*Ibid.*, 13: Ingenium mala saepe movent (Crosses ofttimes bestir the wit).

Horace, *Sat.*, ii, 8, 73–74: Ingenium res adversae nudare solent, celare secundae (Mishaps often reveal genius, smooth going hides it). ¶Ovid, *Artis Amat.*, ii, 43: Ingenium mala saepe movent (Ills often stir the wits).

Cf. Tilley, *Prov. in Eng.*, C15a.

21   DO NOT TORMENT YOUR MIND WITH CARES

Rich. II, III, iv, 2: Drive away the heavy thought of care.

Culman, 22: Ne curis tuum ipsius animum excrucies (Do not torment thy mind with cares).

22   WHEN THE CAT'S AWAY, THE MICE WILL PLAY

Hen. V, I, ii, 172: Playing the mouse in absence of the cat.

Culman, 19: Dum felis dormit, saliunt mures (Whilst the cat sleepeth the mice skip about).

Cf. Tilley, *Prov. in Eng.*, C175.

23   ALL THINGS CHANGE

Rom. & Jul., IV, v, 90: All things change them to the contrary. ¶*Jul. Caesar*, I, iii, 66–67: All . . . things change from their ordinance, Their natures, and preformed faculties.

Culman, 3: Omnia mutantur (All things are changed). ¶*Ibid.*, 9: Tempore omnia mutantur (All things are changed in time). ¶*Ibid.*, 14: Omnes res facile mutantur (All things are quickly changed). ¶*Ibid.*, 22: Mortalia omnia mutationes multas habent (All mortal things have many changes).

Aristotle, *Politics*, v, 10, 1 : τὸ μὴ μένειν μηθὲν ἀλλ' ἔν τινι περιόδῳ μεταβάλλειν (Nothing is permanent, but everything changes). ¶Ovid, *Metam.*, xv, 165 : Omnia mutantur (All things are changing). ¶Erasmus, *Adagia*, 286A: Omnium rerum vicissitudo est (In all things there is change).
Cf. Taverner, 22; Tilley, *Prov. in Eng.*, C233.

24   CHASTITY (MODESTY) IS A WOMAN'S DOWRY

Hamlet, III, i, 140–141 : Plague for thy dowry: be thou as chaste as ice, as pure as snow. ¶*All's Well*, II, iii, 150–151 : Virtue and she Is her own dower. ¶*Tempest*, III, i, 53–54: My [Miranda] modesty (The jewel in my dower).
Culman, 7: Mulieris dos pudicitia (Chastity is a woman's dowry).

25   ONCE A MAN AND TWICE A CHILD

Lucrece, 939–954: Time's glory is . . . To make the child a man, the man a child. ¶*As You Like It*, II, vii, 163–165: Last scene of all, That ends this strange eventful history, Is second childishness and mere oblivion. ¶*Hamlet*, II, ii, 403: They say an old man is twice a child. ¶*K. Lear*, I, iii, 19: Old fools are babes again. ¶*Pericles*, IV, iii, 3–4: I think You'll turn a child again. ¶*Cymb.*, V, iii, 57: Two boys, an old man (twice a boy).
Culman, 5: Bis pueri senes (Old men are twice children).
Aristophanes, *The Clouds*, 1417: ἐγὼ δέ γ' ἀντείποιμ' ἂν ὡς δὶς παῖδες οἱ γέροντες (I would reply that old men are twice boys). ¶Plautus, *Mercator*, 295–296: Senex quom extemplo est, iam nec sentit nec sapit, aiunt solere eum rusum repuerascere (Once a man gets old and reaches the senseless, witless stage, they do say he's apt to have a second childhood). ¶Erasmus, *Adagia*, 195B: Bis pueri senes (Twice a boy, once an old man).
Cf. Taverner, 16; Smith, 472; Tilley, *Prov. in Eng.*, M570.

26   CHILDREN ARE THE BLESSING OF GOD

All's Well, I, iii, 26–28: I think I shall never have the blessing of God till I have issue o' my body; for they say barnes are blessings.

Culman, 33: Liberorum copia, Dei donum optimum (Store of children is a very good gift of God).

Cicero, *Post Reditum*, i, 1, 2: Quid dulcius hominum generi ab natura datum est quam sui cuique liberi (Of all nature's gifts to the human race, what is sweeter to a man than his children)?

Cf. Tilley, *Prov. in Eng.*, C331.

27   CHILDREN SHOULD NOT BE EXPOSED
TO WICKEDNESS

Merry Wives, II, ii, 133–134: 'Tis not good that children should know any wickedness.

Culman, 36: Scandalum non praestandum pueris (Children ought not to be exposed to sin).

28   BE CLEANLY

Winter's T., I, ii, 123: We must be neat—not neat, but cleanly.

Culman, 2: Mundus esto (Be cleanly).

Cato, *Collectio Dis. Vulg.*, 8: Mundus esto (Be tidy).

29   CLEMENCY (COURTESY, PITY) BREEDS
GOOD WILL AND FAVOR

Pericles, IV, ii, 131–132: Pity begets you a good opinion, and that opinion a mere profit.

* Publilius Syrus (1934), 90: Bona comparat praesidia misericordia (Pity provides good defenses). ¶ *Ibid.*, 370: Misereri scire sine periclo est vivere (To know how to pity is to live without danger).

Seneca, *De Clem.*, i, 11, 4: Clementia ergo non tantum honestiores sed tutiores praestat ornamentumque imperiorum est simul et certissima salus (Mercy, then, makes rulers not only more honored, but safer, and is at the same time the glory of sovereign power and its surest protection).

30   IN TROUBLE (MISERY) IT IS GOOD TO HAVE **COMPANY**

Titus Andr. (Q.2 and Ff.), V, iii, 169: Friends should associate friends in grief and woe. ¶*Lucrece*, 790: Fellowship in woe doth woe assuage. ¶*Ibid.*, 1111–1113: Grief best is pleas'd with grief's society; True sorrow then is feelingly suffic'd When with like semblance it is sympathiz'd. ¶*L. Lab. Lost*, IV, iii, 49: In love, I hope—sweet fellowship in shame. ¶*Ibid.*, 127–128: Thy love is far from charity, That in love's grief desir'st society. ¶*Rom. & Jul.*, III, ii, 116: Sour woe delights in fellowship. ¶*K. Lear*, III, vi, 110–113: Who alone suffers suffers most i' th' mind, . . . the mind much sufferance doth o'erskip When grief hath mates, and bearing fellowship. ¶*Winter's T.*, I, ii, 190–196: There have been . . . cuckolds ere now . . . there's comfort in 't.

Culman, 26: Solatium in miseriis amicus compatiens (A friend that suffers with us, is a comfort in miseries). ¶Publilius Syrus (1835), 1012: Calamitatum habere socios miseris est solatio (It is a consolation to the wretched to have companions in misery).

Cato, *Collectio Monos.*, 63: Quisque miser casu alterius solatia sumit (Another's woe consoles all wretched folk). ¶Seneca, *Ad Marciam de Con.*, xii, 5: Solacii genus est turba miserorum (A crowd of fellow sufferers is a kind of comfort in misery). ¶Erasmus, *Epist.*, 427E: Societas miseriam levat (Fellowship lightens misery).

Cf. Tilley, *Eliz. Prov. Lore*, 446, *Prov. in Eng.*, C571.

31   KEEP NOT ILL **COMPANY** LEST YOU INCREASE THE NUMBER

2 Hen. IV, V, i, 72–76: It is a wonderful thing to see the semblable coherence of his men's spirits and his. They, by observing of him, do bear themselves like foolish justices; he, by conversing with them, is turned into a justice-like servingman.

Culman, 12: Fies malus malorum contubernio (Thou shalt be made evil by the company of evil men). ¶ *Ibid.*, 27: Talis quisque fit, cum qualibus habet familiaritatem (Everyone becomes such as they with whom he is familiar).
Cf. Tilley, *Prov. in Eng.*, M536.

32 COMPARISONS ARE ODIOUS

Much Ado, III, v, 18: Comparisons are odorous.
Culman, 5: Comparatio omnis odiosa (Every comparison is odious).
Cf. Tilley, *Eliz. Prov. Lore*, 111, *Prov. in Eng.*, C576; Baldwin, I, 591.

33 CONFESSION OF A FAULT PARDONS IT

Merry Wives, I, i, 107: If it be confessed, it is not redressed.
Publilius Syrus (1835), 1079: Proximum tenet locum confessio innocentiae (Confession of our faults is the next thing to innocence).
Cf. Tilley, *Prov. in Eng.*, C590.

34 BE ABLE TO CONQUER YOUR ENEMY,
BUT SPARE HIM

Cf. no. 147: To be able to do harm and to abstain from doing it is noble
All's Well, I, i, 74–75: Be able for thine enemy Rather in power than use.
Publilius Syrus (1934), 686: Satis est superare inimicum, nimium est perdere (It is enough to vanquish a foe, too much to ruin him).
Statius, *Thebaidos*, vi, 816: Pulchrum vitam donare minori (It is noble to spare the vanquished).

35 CONSCIENCE IS A THOUSAND WITNESSES

Rich. III, V, ii, 17–18: Every man's conscience is a thousand men, To fight against this guilty homicide. ¶ *Ibid.*, iii, 194–196: My conscience hath a thousand several tongues, And every tongue brings in a several tale, And every tale condemns me for a villain.

Culman, 5: Conscientia mille testes (Conscience is a thousand witnesses).

Quintilian, *Inst. Orat.*, v, 11, 41: Conscientia mille testes (Conscience is as good as a thousand witnesses). ¶Erasmus, *Adagia*, 394D: Conscientia mille testes (Conscience is worth a thousand witnesses).

Cf. Taverner, 27; Bacon, *Promus*, 998; Tilley, *Prov. in Eng.*, C601.

36   A BAD **CONSCIENCE** IS A SILENT TORTURE OF THE MIND

Rich. III, I, iii, 222: The worm of conscience still begnaw thy soul! ¶ *Merry Wives*, III, iii, 234: You suffer for a pad conscience. ¶ *Troilus & Cres.*, V, x, 28–29: I'll haunt thee like a wicked conscience still, That mouldeth goblins swift as frenzy's thoughts.

Publilius Syrus (1934), 490: O tacitum tormentum animi conscientia (O conscience, silent torture of the mind)! ¶*Ibid.* (1835), 739: Quam conscientia animi gravis est servitus (How oppressive is the weight of an evil conscience)!

37   A GOOD **CONSCIENCE** IS VERY PLEASANT

2 Hen. IV, Epil., 21–22: A good conscience will make any possible satisfaction.

Culman, 11 · Conscientia recta suavissima est (A good conscience is very sweet).

38   IT IS AN OFFENSE TO **CONTROL** A MAN AGAINST HIS WILL

Much Ado, III, iii, 88: It is an offence to stay a man against his will.

Publilius Syrus (1934), 436: Non corrigit, sed laedit, qui invitum regit (He who controls the unwilling hurts rather than corrects).

39 TAKE **COUNSEL** OF THE WISE

Cf. no. 171: Learn from the learned
Pass. Pilgr., 18, 5: Take counsel of some wiser head.
Culman, 18: Consilium petendum a consultis & prudentibus
(Counsel is to be asked of men that are advised and discreet).

40 **COURAGE** MOUNTS WITH OCCASION

Cf. no. 41: In great danger courage counts for most
K. John, II, i, 82: For courage mounteth with occasion. ¶ *Troilus &
Cres.*, I, iii, 33–34: In the reproof of chance Lies the true proof of men.
Publilius Syrus (1934), 447: Non novit virtus calamitati cedere
(Bravery knows no yielding to calamity).
Lucan, *De Bello Civili*, iii, 614: Crevit in adversis virtus (His courage
rose with disaster).
Cf. Tilley, *Prov. in Eng.*, C715.

41 IN GREAT DANGER **COURAGE** COUNTS FOR MOST

Cf. no. 40: Courage mounts with occasion
Hen. V, IV, i, 1–2: 'Tis true that we are in great danger; The greater
therefore should our courage be.
Publilius Syrus (1934), 227: Felicitatem in dubiis virtus impetrat
(Valour secures success in hazards). ¶ * *Ibid.*, 298: In rebus dubiis
plurimi est audacia (In a tight corner boldness counts for most).

42 FULL OF **COURTESY**, FULL OF CRAFT

Rich. III, I, iii, 289–290: Take heed of yonder dog! Look, when he
fawns he bites. ¶ *Jul. Caesar*, IV, ii, 20–21: When love begins to sicken
and decay It useth an enforced ceremony. ¶ *Timon*, I, ii, 15–18: Nay,
my lords, ceremony was but devis'd at first To set a gloss on faint

deeds, hollow welcomes, Recanting goodness, sorry ere 'tis shown; But where there is true friendship, there needs none. ❡ *Pericles*, I, iv, 75: Who makes the fairest show means most deceit.

Culman, 11: Cum blanditur inimicus fallit (An enemy deceiveth when he flattereth).

Cf. Tilley, *Prov. in Eng.*, C732.

43 ALL **COVET**, ALL LOSE

1 Hen. VI, V, iv, 144–146: I'll rather keep That which I have than, coveting for more, Be cast from possibility of all.

Culman, 35: Qui plus ambit, minus consequitur (He that coveteth to get more, getteth less).

Cf. Tilley, *Prov. in Eng.*, A127.

44 LOSE **CREDIT** AND ONE CAN LOSE NO MORE

Rich. II, I, i, 182–183: Mine honour is my life. Both grow in one; Take honour from me, and my life is done. ❡ *Othello*, II, iii, 262–265: Reputation, reputation, reputation! O, I have lost my reputation! I have lost the immortal part of myself, and what remains is bestial.

* Publilius Syrus (1934), 209: Fidem qui perdit nihil pote ultra perdere (Lose credit and one can lose no more).

Cf. Tilley, *Prov. in Eng.*, C817.

45 **CROSSES** HASTEN OLD AGE

Rom. & Jul., III, ii, 89: These griefs, these woes, these sorrows make me old. ❡ *Ibid.*, V, iii, 212: What further woe conspires against mine age?

Culman, 7: Mala senium accelerant (Crosses hasten old age).

Erasmus, *Adagia*, 943A: Mala senium accelerant (Adversities hasten old age).

46   A MAN IN HIS CUPS WILL TELL HIS MIND

Much Ado, III, iii, 111–112: I will, like a true drunkard, utter all to thee.

Culman, 12: Ebrietas abditissima pectoris profert (Drunkenness doth discover the greatest secrets of the mind).

Ovid, *Tristia*, iii, 5, 48: Lapsaque sunt nimio verba profana mero (Let slip no impious words by reason of too much wine). ¶ Plutarch, *Moralia*: *On Garrulity*, 503F: ἐν τῇ καρδίᾳ τοῦ νήφοντος ἐπὶ τῆς γλώττης ἐστὶ τοῦ μεθύοντος, ὡς οἱ παροιμιαζόμενοί φασιν (What is in a man's heart when he is sober is on his tongue when he is drunk, as those who are given to proverbs say). ¶ Erasmus, *Adagia*, 428D: Quod in animo sobrii, id est in lingua ebrii (What is in a sober man's mind is on the tongue of a drunkard); cf. 267B.

Cf. Bacon, *Promus*, 999.

47   WHAT CANNOT BE CURED MUST BE ENDURED

Cf. no. 7: What cannot be altered must be borne, not blamed (lamented);
    no. 105: It is folly to fear what cannot be avoided

Two Gent., II, ii, 1–2: Have patience, gentle Julia. —I must, where is no remedy. ¶ *Much Ado*, I, iii, 9–10: If not a present remedy, at least a patient sufferance. ¶ *Merry Wives*, V, v, 251: What cannot be eschew'd must be embrac'd.

Culman, 24: Patienter ferenda quae mutari non possunt (Those things which cannot be altered are to be patiently borne). ¶ Publilius Syrus (1934), 411: Mutare quod non possis, ut natum est, feras (What you cannot change, you should bear as it comes).

Seneca, *Epist.*, cvii, 9: Optimum est pati, quod emendare non possis (That which you cannot reform, it is best to endure).

Cf. Tilley, *Prov. in Eng.*, C922.

48   CUSTOM MAKES ALL THINGS EASY

As You Like It, II, i, 2–3: Hath not old custom made this life more sweet Than that of painted pomp? ¶ *Hamlet*, V, i, 76: Custom hath made it in him a property of easiness. ¶ *Othello*, I, iii, 230–232: The tyrant custom . . . Hath made the flinty and steel couch of war My thrice-driven bed of down. ¶*Coriol.*, II, iii, 124–126: Custom calls me to't. What custom wills, in all things should we do't, The dust on antique time would lie unswept.

Culman, 11: Consuetudo omnia dura lenit (Custom doth make all hard things easy).

Cf. Tilley, *Prov. in Eng.*, C933.

49   CUSTOM MAKES SIN NO SIN

Hamlet, III, iv, 37–38: If damned custom have not braz'd it so That it is proof and bulwark against sense. ¶*Ibid.*, 161–162: That monster, custom, who all sense doth eat Of habits evil. ¶*Pericles*, I, Prol., 29–30: By custom what they did begin Was with long use account'd no sin. ¶*Winter's T.*, IV, iv, 10–13: But that our feasts In every mess have folly, and the feeders Digest it with a custom, I should blush To see you so attir'd.

Culman, 10: Assueta mala non offendunt (Evils that one is used to do not offend).

Cf. Tilley, *Eliz. Prov. Lore*, 753, *Prov. in Eng.*, C934.

50   THE SWAY OF CUSTOM IS TYRANNOUS

Othello, I, iii, 230: The tyrant custom.

* Publilius Syrus (1934), 236: Gravissimum est imperium consuetudinis (Most tyrannous is the sway of custom).

51 NO DANGER INCURRED, NO DANGER REPELLED

All's Well, I, i, 239–241: Impossible be strange attempts to those That weigh their pains in sense, and do suppose What hath been cannot be. ¶*Meas. for Meas.*, I, iv, 77–79: Our doubts are traitors And make us lose the good we oft might win By fearing to attempt.

* Publilius Syrus (1934), 428: Numquam periclum sine periclo vincitur (A risk is never mastered save by risk).

52   **DEATH** IS COMMON TO ALL

Hamlet, I, ii, 72: Thou know'st 'tis common. All that lives must die.

Culman, 14: Mors omni aetati communis est (Death is common to every age).

Homer, *Odyssey*, iii, 236: θάνατον μὲν ὁμοίιον (Death which is common to all). ¶Sophocles, *Electra*, 860: πᾶσι θνατοῖς ἔφυ μόρος (Death is the common lot); cf. 1173. ¶Cato, *Collectio Monos.*, 3: Mors omnibus una (Death is one for all). ¶Erasmus, *Adagia*, 923B: Mors omnibus communis (Death is common to all).

Cf. Udall, *Apoph. of Erasm.*, 23:52; Tilley, *Prov. in Eng.*, D142.

53   **DEATH** IS THE END OF ALL MISERY

Com. of Errors, I, i, 2: By the doom of death end woes and all. ¶*1 Hen. VI*, II, v, 28–29: The arbitrator of despairs, Just Death, kind umpire of men's miseries. ¶*Ibid.*, III, ii, 136–137: Kings and mightiest potentates must die, For that's the end of human misery. ¶*Rich. II*, II, i, 152: Though death be poor, it ends a mortal woe. ¶*K. Lear*, IV, vi, 61–62: Is wretchedness depriv'd that benefit To end itself by death? ¶*Timon*, IV, iii, 248: Thou shouldst desire to die, being miserable.

Culman, 6: Finis miseriae mors (Death is the end of misery). ¶*Publilius Syrus (1934), 67: Bona mors est homini vitae quae exstinguit mala (Good for man is death when it ends life's miseries). ¶*Ibid.*, 672: Spes inopem, res avarum, mors miserum levat (Hope eases the beggar, wealth the miser, death the wretched).

Cato, *Disticha*, iii, 22: Quae [mors] bona si non est, finis tamen illa malorum est (Death, if no boon, is the end of our evils). ¶Cicero, *Tusc. Disp.*, i, 42, 100: Vitae miserae mors finis esse videtur (Death seems to be the end of a wretched life). ¶Seneca, *Ad Marciam de Con.*, xix, 5: Mors dolorum omnium exsolutio est et finis (Death is a release from, and the end of, all suffering).

54   **DEATH** IS THE GRAND LEVELER

Hamlet, IV, iii, 24–26: Your fat king and your lean beggar is but variable service—two dishes, but to one table. That's the end. ¶*Meas.*

for Meas., III, i, 40–41: Death . . . makes these odds all even. ¶*Cymb.*, IV, ii, 252–253: Thersites' body is as good as Ajax' When neither are alive.

Culman, 7: Mors omnia sternit (Death throws down all afore it). ¶Publilius Syrus (1835), 1: A morte semper homines tantumdem absumus (As men, we are all equal in the presence of death). Seneca, *Ad Marciam de Con.*, xx, 1–2: Mors . . . exaequat omnia (Death levels all things). ¶Seneca, *De Ira*, iii, 43, 2: Mors . . . vos pares faciat (Death will make you equals). ¶Seneca, *Epist.*, xcix, 9: Exitu aequamur (Death levels us). ¶Claudian, *De Raptu Proserpinae*, ii, 302: Omnia mors aequat (Death levels all things).

Cf. Tilley, *Prov. in Eng.*, D143.

55   AN HONORABLE **DEATH** IS BETTER THAN A SHAMEFUL LIFE

1 Hen. VI, I, iv, 31–33: Once in contempt they would have barter'd me; Which I disdaining scorn'd, and craved death Rather than I would be so vile esteem'd. ¶*Ibid.*, IV, v, 32–33: Here on my knee I beg mortality Rather than life preserv'd with infamy. ¶*Lucrece*, 1186: 'Tis honour to deprive dishonour'd life. ¶*Hen. V*, IV, v, 23: Let life be short; else shame will be too long. ¶*Coriol.*, I, vi, 71: Brave death outweighs bad life.

Culman, 24: Praestat mori, quam foedam vitam vivere (It is better to die than to lead a dishonest life). ¶Publilius Syrus (1835), 331: Honestam mortem vitae turpi praefero (An honorable death is better than a disgraceful life). ¶*Ibid.*, 1102: Tolerabilior, qui mori jubet, quam qui male vivere (A sentence to death is more tolerable than a command to live wickedly).

Claudian, *De Bello Gild.*, i, 451: Nonne mori satius, vitae quam ferre pudorem (Is not death preferable to a life disgraced)? ¶Tacitus, *Agricola*, 33: Honesta mors turpi vita potior (Honorable death is better than dishonorable life). ¶Juvenal, *Sat.*, viii, 83: Summum crede nefas animam praeferre pudori (Count it the greatest of all sins to prefer life to honor).

Cf. Tilley, *Eliz. Prov. Lore*, 143, *Prov. in Eng.*, H576.

56   AS CERTAIN AS **DEATH**

Cf. no. 67: All men must die

Titus Andr., I, i, 486: And sure as death. ¶*Rich. II*, III, ii, 103: Death will have his day. ¶*2 Hen. IV*, III, ii, 41–42: Death, as the Psalmist saith, is certain to all. ¶*Ibid.*, 45: Death is certain. ¶*Jul. Caesar*, II, ii, 36–37: Death, a necessary end, Will come when it will come. ¶*Ibid.*, III, i, 99: That we shall die, we know. ¶*All's Well*, II, iii, 20: Uncertain life, and sure death. ¶*Two Noble K.*, V, iv, 18: To us death is certain.
Culman, 7: Mors est inevitabilis (Death is unavoidable).
Plautus, *Captivi*, 732: Non moriri certius (Fixed as death).
Cf. Tilley, *Prov. in Eng.*, D136.

57   THE FEAR OF **DEATH** IS WORSE THAN
                    DEATH ITSELF

Meas. for Meas., III, i, 78: The sense of death is most in apprehension. ¶*Ibid.*, V, i, 399–403: Death ... is better life, past fearing death, Than that which lives to fear.
Publilius Syrus (1835), 520: Mortem timere crudelius est quam mori (The fear of death is more to be dreaded than death itself).
Cf. Stevenson, 516:2.

58   WHEN TO LIVE IS TORMENT, **DEATH** IS BEST

Two Gent., III, i, 170: And why not death rather than living torment? ¶*Othello*, I, iii, 309–310: It is silliness to live when to live is torment.
Publilius Syrus (1934), 465: Nemo immature moritur qui moritur miser (None dies untimely who dies in misery). ¶*Ibid.*, 701: Ubi omnis vitae metus est, mors est optima (When life is all one terror, death is best).

59   NOBLE **DEEDS** DIE, IF SUPPRESSED IN SILENCE

Winter's T., I, ii, 92–93: One good deed dying tongueless Slaughters a thousand.

Publilius Syrus (1934), 304: Iacet omnis virtus fama nisi late patet (Every virtue is depressed unless it gains wide recognition).

Pindar, *Eulogy on Alex.*, 121: θνᾴσκει δὲ σιγαθὲν καλὸν ἔργον (Every noble deed dies, if suppressed in silence).

60   NOBLE MINDS, NOBLE DEEDS

Pericles, II, v, 59: My actions are as noble as my thoughts.

Culman, 25: Probis ab animis facta promanant proba (Honest deeds proceed from honest minds).

61   IT IS HARD TO RESTORE ONE WHOM ILL REPORT HAS ONCE DEGRADED

Hamlet, I, iv, 30–38: These men Carrying, I say, the stamp of one defect, . . . be they as pure as grace, . . . Shall in the general censure take corruption From that particular fault. The dram of e'il Doth all the noble substance often dout To his own scandal.

Publilius Syrus (1934), 572: Quem fama semel oppressit vix restituitur (It is hard restoring him whom ill report has once crushed).

Cato, *Collectio Monos.*, 5: Numquam sanantur deformis vulnera famae (The wounds of base repute are never cured). ¶ Spenser, *F. Q.*, VI, vi, 1, 3–6: The poysnous sting, which infamy Infixeth in the name of noble wight . . . by no art, nor any leaches might It euer can recured be againe.

62   UNLESS DEGREE IS PRESERVED, THE HIGHEST PLACE IS SAFE FOR NO ONE

Troilus & Cres., I, iii, 101–108: When degree is shak'd, . . . Then enterprise is sick! How could communities, . . . crowns, sceptres, laurels, But by degree, stand in authentic place?

Publilius Syrus (1934), 476: Ni gradus servetur, nulli tutus est summus locus (Unless degree is preserved, the highest place is safe for no one).

63   A LITTLE **DELAY** SEEMS VERY LONG

As You Like It, III, ii, 206–207: One inch of delay more is a South Sea of discovery.

Culman, 23: Omnis mora, quantumvis pusilla, longissima videtur (All delay, though it be very little, doth seem very long).

Seneca, *Agamemnon*, 426: Omnisque nimium longa properanti mora est (All delay is too long to one who is in haste).

64   WE **DESIRE** WHAT IS FORBIDDEN

Meas. for Meas., I, ii, 132–134: Our natures do pursue, Like rats that ravin down their proper bane, A thirsty evil.

Culman, 10: Vetita magis appetimus (We lust more after things forbidden). ¶ Publilius Syrus (1934), 438: Nihil magis amat cupiditas quam quod non licet (Longing desire likes nothing better than what is not allowed).

Ovid, *Amores*, ii, 19, 3: Quod licet, ingratum est; quod non licet acrius urit (What one may do freely has no charm; what one may not do pricks more keenly on). ¶ *Ibid.*, iii, 4, 25: Quidquid servatur cupimus magis, . . . pauci, quod sinit alter, amant (Whatever is guarded we desire the more; few love what another concedes). ¶ Seneca, *Hercules Oetaeus*, 357: Illicita amantur (What is forbidden we love).

Cf. Tilley, *Eliz. Prov. Lore*, 258, *Prov. in Eng.*, F585; Stevenson, 1893:10.

65   WE **DESPISE** THINGS THAT ARE PRESENT

2 Hen. IV, I, iii, 108: Past, and to come, seems best; things present, worst.

Culman, 27: Spernimus in commune omnes praesentia (We all in common despise things that are present).

66   THE DOOM OF **DESTINY** CANNOT BE AVOIDED

Cf. no. 120: In all human affairs fortune (providence) rules

3 Hen. VI, IV, iii, 58: What fates impose, that men must needs abide. ¶ *Rich. III*, IV, iv, 218: All unavoided is the doom of destiny. ¶ *Jul.*

Caesar, II, ii, 26–27: What can be avoided Whose end is purpos'd by the mighty gods? ¶*Coriol.*, II, ii, 116: Shunless destiny.

Culman, 26: Quod fatis decretum est, id nemini licet evitare (What the destinies have decreed, no man can avoid).

Homer, *Iliad*, vi, 488: μοῖραν δ' οὔ τινά φημι πεφυγμένον ἔμμεναι ἀνδρῶν (No man has ever escaped his destiny). ¶Sophocles, *Antigone*, 1106: ἀνάγκη δ' οὐχὶ δυσμαχητέον (To war with destiny is vain). ¶Euripides, *Rhesus*, 634: οὐκ ἂν δύναιο τοῦ πεπρωμένου πλέον (Thou canst not overpass the doom of fate); cf. *Hercules*, 311; *Hippolytus*, 1256.

Cf. Stevenson, 555:7; Tilley, *Prov. in Eng.*, F83.

67   ALL MEN MUST **DIE**

Cf. no. 56: As certain as death

3 Hen. VI, V, ii, 28: And, live we how we can, yet die we must. ¶*1 Hen. VI*, III, ii, 136: Kings and mightiest potentates must die. ¶*Rom. & Jul.*, III, iii, 92: Death's the end of all. ¶*Ibid.*, iv, 4: We were born to die. ¶*2 Hen. IV*, III, ii, 42: All shall die. ¶*Much Ado*, I, i, 59–60: We are all mortal. ¶*Jul. Caesar*, IV, iii, 190–192: We must die, Messala. With meditating that she must die once, I have the patience to endure it now. ¶*Hamlet*, I, ii, 72: All that lives must die. ¶*Meas. for Meas.*, II, iv, 35–36: Yet may he live awhile; and, it may be, As long as you or I. Yet he must die.

* Publilius Syrus (1934), 360: Mori necesse est, sed non quotiens volueris (You needs must die, but not as often as you have wished). ¶*Ibid.* (1835), 522: Morti debetur, quicquid usquam nascitur (Everything which has birth, must pay tribute to death).

Pindar, *Olympian Odes*, i, 82: θανεῖν δ' οἷσιν ἀνάγκα (All men must die). ¶Cicero, *Tusc. Disp.*, i, 5, 9: Moriendum est enim omnibus (For all men have to die). ¶Cicero, *De Sen.*, xx, 74: Moriendum enim certe est (For it is certain that we must die). ¶Horace, *Odes*, i, 4, 13–14: Pallida Mors aequo pulsat pede pauperum tabernas regumque turres (Pale death with foot impartial knocks at the poor man's cottage and at princes' palaces). ¶Seneca, *Epist.*, lxxvii, 11: Nemo tam imperitus est, ut nesciat quandoque moriendum (No one is so ignorant as not to know that we must at some time die).

Cf. Tilley, *Prov. in Eng.*, M505.

68   PRACTICE **DILIGENCE**

Tempest, I, ii, 304: Go! Hence with diligence!
  Culman, 1: Diligentiam adhibe (Use diligence).
  Cato, *Collectio Dis. Vulg.*, 14: Diligentiam adhibe (Practice diligence).

69   KINGDOMS DECAY BY **DISCORD**

1 Hen. VI, III, i, 72–73: Civil dissension is a viperous worm That gnaws
the bowels of the commonwealth.
  Culman, 5: Discordia dilabuntur regna (Kingdoms decay by discord).

70   A DESPERATE **DISEASE** MUST HAVE A
                 DESPERATE REMEDY

Lucrece, 1337: Extremity still urgeth such extremes. ¶*Rom. & Jul.*, II,
Prol., 13–14: Passion lends them power, time means, to meet, Temp'ring
extremities with extreme sweet. ¶*Ibid.*, IV, i, 68–70: I do spy a kind of
hope, Which craves as desperate an execution As that is desperate which
we would prevent. ¶*Much Ado*, IV, i, 253: To strange sores strangely
they strain the cure. ¶*Hamlet*, IV, iii, 9–11: Diseases desperate grown
By desperate appliance are reliev'd, Or not at all. ¶*Macb.*, IV, iii, 214–
215: Let's make us med'cines of our great revenge To cure this deadly
grief.
  Publilius Syrus (1835), 849: Remedio amaro amaram bilem diluunt
(We get rid of bitter bile with bitter medicines).
  Cicero, *De Offic.*, i, 24, 83: Gravioribus autem morbis periculosas
curationes et ancipites adhibere coguntur (In cases of dangerous sick-
ness they are compelled to apply hazardous and even desperate
remedies).
  Cf. Smith, 137; Tilley, *Prov. in Eng.*, D357.

71 IT IS EASY TO FIND A STAFF TO BEAT A **DOG**

2 Hen. VI, III, i, 170–171: The ancient proverb will be well effected—
'A staff is quickly found to beat a dog.'

Culman, 19: Facile fustem invenerit, qui cupit caedere canem (He will quickly find a cudgel that hath a mind to beat a dog).
Cf. Tilley, *Prov. in Eng.*, T138.

72 A COWARDLY **DOG** BARKS MORE VEHEMENTLY THAN IT BITES

Hen. V, II, iv, 69–71: Coward dogs Most spend their mouths when what they seem to threaten Runs far before them.

Culman, 11: Canes timidi vehementius latrant (Fearful dogs do bark the more eagerly).

Quintus Curtius, *Hist. Alex. Magni*, vii, 4, 13: Adicit deinde, quod apud Bactrianos vulgo usurpabant, canem timidum vehementius latrare quam mordere (Then he added a proverb in common use among the Bactriani, that a timid dog barks more violently than it bites).
¶ Erasmus, *Adagia*, 908B: Canes timidi vehementius latrant (Fearful dogs bark more ferociously).

Cf. Taverner, 62; Stevenson, 613:11; Tilley, *Prov. in Eng.*, D528.

73 EVERYTHING IS EASY AFTER IT HAS BEEN **DONE**

Meas. for Meas., IV, ii, 221–222: All difficulties are but easy when they are known.

Culman, 6: Factum stultus agnoscit (A fool doth own the thing done). ¶ *Ibid.*, 15: Rem peractam stultus intelligit (A fool understands a thing when it is done and past).

Erasmus, *Adagia*, 38C: Factum stultus cognoscit (A fool knows a thing when it has been done).

Cf. Tilley, *Prov. in Eng.*, D418.

74 WHAT'S **DONE** CANNOT BE UNDONE

Titus Andr., IV, ii, 73–74: Villain, what hast thou done?—That which thou canst not undo. ¶ *Rich. III*, IV, iv, 291: What is done cannot be now amended. ¶ *Jul. Caesar*, IV, ii, 8–9: Some worthy cause to wish

Things done undone. ❡ *Merry Wives* (Q.), V, v, 144: 'Tis done sir now, and cannot be undone. ❡ *Macb.*, V, i, 75: What's done cannot be undone. ❡ *Pericles*, IV, iii, 1–6: Why are you foolish? Can it be undone? . . . —Were I chief lord of all this spacious world, I'd give it to undo the deed.

Culman, 26: Quod factum est, infectum fieri non potest (What is done cannot be undone).

Sophocles, *Ajax*, 378: οὐ γὰρ γένοιτ' ἂν ταῦθ' ὅπως οὐχ ὧδ' ἔχειν (What's done is done and nothing can alter it); cf. *Trachiniae*, 742–743. ❡ Plautus, *Aulularia*, 741: Factum est illud: fieri infectum non potest (It's done, and it can't be undone). ❡ Cicero, *Pro Rabirio Postumo*, ix, 26: Mutari factum iam nullo modo poterat (But what was done could not be undone). ❡ Erasmus, *Adagia*, 513C: Quod factum est, infectum fieri non potest (What has been done cannot be undone).

Cf. Taverner, 33; Bacon, *Promus*, 951; Tilley, *Prov. in Eng.*, T200.

75 HE THAT CASTS ALL **DOUBTS** SHALL NEVER BE RESOLVED

Hamlet, IV, iv, 39–44: Now, whether it be . . . some craven scruple Of thinking too precisely on th' event . . . I do not know Why yet I live to say 'This thing's to do.'

Publilius Syrus (1934), 266: Homini tum deest consilium cum multa invenit (When you discover many openings, you are gravelled for a plan).

Cf. Tilley, *Eliz. Prov. Lore*, 623, *Prov. in Eng.*, D571.

76 **DRUNKENNESS** MAKES MEN MAD

Twelfth N., I, v, 139–141: A fool, and a madman. One draught above heat makes him a fool, the second mads him, and a third drowns him.

Culman, 1: Ebrietas dementat (Drunkenness makes men mad).

Seneca, *Epist.*, lxxxiii, 18: Dic . . . nihil aliud esse ebrietatem quam voluntariam insaniam (Say that drunkenness is nothing but madness voluntarily assumed).

77   EVERYONE TAKES DELIGHT IN
HIS OWN **EMPLOYMENT**

Ant. & Cleop., IV, iv, 20–21: To business that we love we rise betime
And go to't with delight.

Culman, 16: Sua quemque studia delectant (His own employments
delight every man). ¶*Ibid.*: Suo quisque studio delectatur (Everyone
is delighted with his own employment).

Ovid, *Ex Ponto*, i, 5, 35–36: Scilicet est cupidus studiorum quisque
suorum, tempus et adsueta ponere in arte iuvat (Clearly each man
shows a passion for his own pursuits, taking pleasure in devoting time
to his familiar art). ¶Erasmus, *Adagia*, 935F: Suo quisque studio
gaudet (Everyone takes delight in his own business).

78   MARK THE **END**

Com. of Errors, IV, iv, 44–46: Mistress, *respice finem*, respect your end;
or rather . . . 'beware the rope's end.' ¶*2 Hen. IV*, II, iv, 303–304:
Well, hearken o' th' end.

Culman, 6: Finem vitae specta (Look at the end of thy life). ¶*Ibid.*,
27: Spectandus semper est finis, & rei exitus (The end and issue of a
thing is ever to be looked at).

Erasmus, *Adagia*, 126D: Finem vitae specta (Mark the end of life).
Cf. Taverner, 50; Tilley, *Prov. in Eng.*, E125.

79   THE **END** CROWNS (TRIES) ALL

2 Hen. VI, V, ii, 28: La fin couronne les oeuvres. ¶*2 Hen. IV*, II, ii,
50–51: Let the end try the man. ¶*All's Well*, IV, iv, 35–36: All's well
that ends well. Still the fine's the crown. Whate'er the course, the end
is the renown. ¶*Ibid.*, V, iii, 336: All is well ended if this suit be won.
¶*Troilus & Cres.*, IV, v, 224: The end crowns all.

Publilius Syrus (1934), 190: Extrema semper de ante factis iudicant
(The end always passes judgment on what has preceded).

Ovid, *Heroides*, ii, 85: Exitus acta probat (The end judges the act).
Cf. Smith, 171; Tilley, *Prov. in Eng.*, E116.

80   THE END OF VILLAINIES IS BASE

K. John, III, i, 88–94: Shame, oppression, perjury . . . all . . . come to ill end.

Culman, 5: Flagitiorum turpis exitus (The end of villainies is base).

Erasmus, *Adagia*, 938A: Flagitiorum turpis exitus (The end of villainies is base).

81   AN ENVIOUS MAN GROWS LEAN

Jul. Caesar, I, ii, 194–209: Yond Cassius has a lean and hungry look . . . Such men as he be never at heart's ease Whiles they behold a greater than themselves.

Culman, 21: Invidus alterius rebus macrescit opimis (An envious man waxeth lean at the prosperity of another).

Horace, *Epist.*, i, 2, 57: Invidus alterius macrescit rebus opimis (The envious man grows lean when his neighbor waxes fat).

Cf. Tilley, *Prov. in Eng.*, M96.

82   EVIL NEVER DIES

Jul. Caesar, III, ii, 81: The evil that men do lives after them.

Culman, 13: Mala herba non perit (An evil weed dieth not).

Sophocles, *Philoctetes*, 446: ἐπεὶ οὐδέν ῾πω κακόν γ' ἀπώλετο (Evil never dies). ¶Erasmus, *Adagia*, 1007D: Malam herbam non perire (The evil weed never dies).

Cf. Stevenson, 715:4; 2476:6.

83   EVIL PROVOKES EVIL

Pericles, I, i, 137: One sin, I know, another doth provoke.

Publilius Syrus (1835), 298: Gradus futuri est, finis praesentis mali (The termination of a present evil is one step toward a future evil).

Homer, *Iliad*, xix, 290: δέχεται κακὸν ἐκ κακοῦ αἰεί (Evil ever follows hard on evil). ¶Terence, *Eunuchus*, 987: Aliud ex alio malum (One evil rises out of another)! ¶Erasmus, *Adagia*, 333C: Noxa item noxam parit (One crime leads to another).

Cf. Stevenson, 712:9; Tilley, *Prov. in Eng.*, E196.

84   IN ALL **EVIL** THERE IS SOMETHING GOOD

Hen. V, IV, i, 4–5: There is some soul of goodness in things evil, Would men observingly distil it out. ¶*Sonnets*, 119, 9–10: O benefit of ill! Now I find true That better is by evil still made better.

Publilius Syrus (1835), 619: Nullum sine auctoramento est magnum malum (There is no great evil which does not bring with it some advantage).

Seneca, *Epist.*, lxix, 4: Nullum sine auctoramento malum est (There is no evil without its compensation).

Cf. Tilley, *Prov. in Eng.*, N328.

85   UNLOOKED-FOR **EVILS** ARE MORE GRIEVOUS

Lucrece, 846–847: O unlook'd-for evil When virtue is profan'd in such a devil! ¶*Rich. II*, I, iii, 154–155: A heavy sentence, my most sovereign liege, And all unlook'd for.

Culman, 13: Inopinata mala graviora sunt (Unlooked for evils are more grievous).

Cicero, *Tusc. Disp.*, iii, 19, 45: Sentit omnia repentina et necopinata esse graviora (He is sensible that the sudden and unexpected is more grievous to bear).

86   **EVIL-GOTTEN** GOODS THRIVE NOT

3 Hen. VI, II, ii, 45–46: Didst thou never hear That things ill got had ever bad success?

Culman, 7: Male partum dilabitur (A thing evil-gotten is quickly gone). ¶*Ibid.*, 16: Turpe lucrum adducit infortunium (Dishonest gain doth bring loss). ¶*Ibid.*, 21: Lucrum malum damnum semper affert (Evil gain always bringeth loss).

Hesiod, *Works and Days*, 352: κακὰ κέρδεα ἶσ’ ἀάτῃσιν (Base gain is as bad as ruin). ¶ Sophocles, *Antigone*, 326: τὰ δειλὰ κέρδη πημονὰς ἐργάζεται (The wages of ill-gotten gains is death). ¶ Plautus, *Poenulus*, 844: Male partum male disperit (Ill-gotten, ill-spent). ¶ Cicero, *Philip.*, ii, 27, 65–66: Sed, ut est apud poetam nescio quem, "Male parta male dilabuntur" (But, as some poet says: "Evil gains come to an evil end"). ¶ Ovid, *Amores*, i, 10, 48: Non habet eventus sordida praeda bonos (A sordid gain can bring no good in the end). ¶ Erasmus, *Adagia*, 294F: Male parta, male dilabuntur (Wickedly gained things wickedly go to ruin).

Cf. Taverner, 23; Tilley, *Prov. in Eng.*, G301.

87   TO **EXCUSE** IS TO ACCUSE

K. John, IV, ii, 30–31: Oftentimes excusing of a fault Doth make the fault the worse by the excuse.

Publilius Syrus (1934), 402: Malam rem cum velis honestare improbes (In wishing to give fair color to a bad case, you condemn it). ¶ *Ibid.*, 420: Multo turpius damnatur cui in delicto ignoscitur (He who is pardoned in his wrong-doing is far more shamefully condemned).

Cf. Tilley, *Prov. in Eng.*, E215.

88   **EXILE** IS A TERRIBLE DEATH

Rom. & Jul., III, iii, 13–14: Exile hath more terror in his look, Much more than death. ¶ *Ibid.*, 43: And sayest thou yet that exile is not death? ¶ *Coriol.*, III, iii, 88–89: Let them pronounce the steep Tarpeian death, Vagabond exile.

* Publilius Syrus (1934), 182: Exsul ubi ei nusquam domus est sine sepulcro est mortuus (The exile with no home anywhere is a corpse without a grave).

89   MAN'S **EXTREMITY** IS GOD'S OPPORTUNITY

K. Lear, IV, vi, 73–74: The clearest gods, who make them honours Of men's impossibilities, have preserv'd thee.

Culman, 30: Deus opitulatur in afflictionibus (God doth help us in afflictions).

Cf. Tilley, *Prov. in Eng.*, M471.

90 BELIEVE YOUR **EYES** RATHER THAN YOUR EARS

Lucrece, 1324–1328: To see sad sights moves more than hear them told; For then the eye interprets to the ear The heavy motion that it doth behold, When every part a part of woe doth bear. 'Tis but a part of sorrow that we hear. ¶ *1 Hen. IV*, V, iv, 139–140: We will not trust our eyes Without our ears. ¶ *Hamlet*, I, i, 56–58: I might not this believe Without the sensible and true avouch Of mine own eyes.

Culman, 15: Oculi auribus sunt fideliores (The eyes are more faithful than the ears). ¶ *Ibid.*, 23: Oculis magis habenda fides, quam auribus (We are rather to believe our eyes than our ears). ¶ Publilius Syrus (1835), 637: Oculis habenda quam auribus est major fides (Put more confidence in your eyes than your ears).

Herodotus, *Hist.*, i, 8: ὦτα γὰρ τυγχάνει ἀνθρώποισι ἐόντα ἀπιστότερα ὀφθαλμῶν (Men trust their ears less than their eyes). ¶ Seneca, *Epist.*, vi, 5: Homines amplius oculis quam auribus credunt (Men put more faith in their eyes than in their ears). ¶ Erasmus, *Adagia*, 67D: Oculis magis habenda fides, quam auribus (Better to trust your eyes than your ears).

Cf. Taverner, 4; Stevenson, 737:9; Tilley, *Prov. in Eng.*, C815.

91   WHERE **FAIR** MEANS MAY NOT PREVAIL, THERE FOUL MEANS RIGHTLY MAY BE USED

2 Hen. VI, IV, ii, 184–185: Seeing gentle words will not prevail, Assail them with the army of the King. ¶ *Ibid.*, V, i, 139–140: Our words will serve. —And if words will not, then our weapons shall.

Publilius Syrus (1934), 605: Quem bono tenere non potueris, contineas malo (Him you have failed to control by fair means, you must restrain by foul).

92   THE **FALLING-OUT** OF LOVERS IS THE
RENEWING OF LOVE

Troilus & Cres., III, i, 112–113: Falling in, after falling out, may make them three. ¶ *Sonnets*, 119, 11–12: Ruin'd love, when it is built anew, Grows fairer than at first, more strong, far greater.

Publilius Syrus (1835), 24: Amantium ira amoris integratio est (The anger of lovers renews the strength of love).

Terence, *Andria*, 555: Amantium irae amoris integratiost (Lovers' quarrels are love's renewal). ¶ Erasmus, *Adagia*, 740C: Amantium irae, amoris redintegratio est (Through the quarrels of lovers is the renewing of love).

Cf. Tilley, *Eliz. Prov. Lore*, 209, *Prov. in Eng.*, F40.

93   **FAME** IS A SPUR TO GREAT DEEDS

Troilus & Cres., II, ii, 199–200: Honour and renown, A spur to valiant and magnanimous deeds.

Culman, 13: Immensum gloria calcar habet (Glory hath a very great spur).

Ovid, *Ex Ponto*, iv, 2, 36: Inmensum gloria calcar habet (Renown possesses a mighty spur). ¶ Spenser, *Tears of the Muses*, 454: Praise . . . is the spur of dooing well. ¶ Lodge, *Robert, Sec. Duke of Normandy, Works* (Hunt. Cl.), II, 16: Honours are the spurres of vertue. ¶ Milton, *Lycidas*, 70: Fame is the spur that the clear spirit doth raise.

94 FAME (A GOOD NAME) IS BETTER THAN RICHES

Rich. II, I, i, 177–178: The purest treasure mortal times afford Is spotless reputation. ¶ *Othello*, III, iii, 157–161: Who steals my purse steals trash . . . But he that filches from me my good name Robs me of that which not enriches him And makes me poor indeed.

Culman, 20: Haereditas famae, quam divitiarum, honestior (The inheritance of a good name is more honest than that of riches). ¶ * Publilius Syrus (1934), 75: Bona opinio hominum tutior pecunia est (There is more safety in men's good opinion than in money). ¶ *Ibid.*,

96: Bene audire alterum patrimonium est (To have a good name is a second patrimony). ¶* *Ibid.*, 254: Honestus rumor alterum est patrimonium (An honorable reputation is a second patrimony). ¶*Ibid.*, 546: Probo bona fama maxima est hereditas (For the upright a good name is the greatest inheritance). ¶*Ibid.* (1835), 328: Honesta fama est alterum patrimonium (A good reputation is a second patrimony).

Old Testament: *Proverbs*, xxii, 1: A good name is rather to be chosen than great riches.

Cf. Tilley, *Prov. in Eng.*, N22.

95   TOO MUCH FAMILIARITY BREEDS CONTEMPT

Merry Wives, I, i, 257–258: I hope upon familiarity will grow more content. ¶*Sonnets*, 102, 12: Sweets grown common lose their dear delight.

Publilius Syrus (1835), 652: Parit contemptum nimia familiaritas (Too much familiarity breeds contempt).

Suetonius, *De Vita Caesarum*, iii, 10, 1: Vitato assiduitatis fastidio (Contempt born of familiarity). ¶Diogenes Laertius, *Heraclitus*, ix, 6: μὴ ἐκ τοῦ δημώδους εὐκαταφρόνητον ᾖ (Lest familiarity should breed contempt).

Cf. Tilley, *Eliz. Prov. Lore*, 211, *Prov. in Eng.*, F47; Stevenson, 756:6.

96   EVERYONE AFTER HIS OWN FANCY

All's Well, IV, i, 19–20: We must everyone be a man of his own fancy.

Culman, 16: Trahit sua quemque voluptas (His own pleasure doth draw on every man).

Cf. Tilley, *Prov. in Eng.*, M100.

97   WHAT YOU FIND FAULT WITH IN OTHERS,
YOU SHOULD NOT BE GUILTY OF

Lucrece, 612–613: With foul offenders thou perforce must bear When they in thee the like offences prove. ¶*L. Lab. Lost*, IV, iii, 131–132: You blush! As his your case is such. You chide at him, offending twice as much. ¶ *Much Ado*, I, i, 290–291: Ere you flout old ends any further, examine your conscience. ¶ *As You Like It*, II, vii, 63–69: What, for a counter, would I do but good? —Most mischievous foul sin, in chiding sin . . . And all th' embossed sores and headed evils That thou with license of free foot hast caught, Wouldst thou disgorge into the general world. ¶ *Meas. for Meas.*, III, ii, 281–282: Shame to him whose cruel striking Kills for faults of his own liking! ¶ *Timon*, V, i, 40–41: Wilt thou whip thine own faults in other men? ¶ *Sonnets*, 152, 5–6: But why of two oaths' breach do I accuse thee When I break twenty?

Culman, 25: Quod aliis vitio vertas, ipse ne feceris (Thou must not do that which thou blamest others for). ¶ Publilius Syrus (1835), 809: Quod aliis vitio vertis, ne ipse admiseris (What you blame in others as a fault, you should not be guilty of yourself).

Aristotle, *Rhet.*, ii, 23, 7: ἄτοπός ἐστιν, ὅταν τις ἐπιτιμᾷ ἄλλοις ἃ αὐτὸς ποιεῖ ἢ ποιήσειεν ἄν (It is ridiculous for a man to reproach others for what he does or would do himself). ¶ Plautus, *Truculentus*, 160: Qui alterum incusat probri, sumpse enitere oportet (He who damns another's faults had best be a paragon himself). ¶ Cato, *Disticha*, i, 30: Quae culpare soles ea tu ne feceris ipse (Do not yourself what you are wont to blame). ¶ Cicero, *Tusc. Disp.*, iii, 30, 73: Est enim proprium stultitiae aliorum vitia cernere, oblivisci suorum (It is a peculiarity of folly to discern the faults of others and be forgetful of its own). ¶ Erasmus, *Adagia*, 926C: Quod aliis vitio vertas, ipse ne feceris (What you find fault with in others, you yourself should not do).

Cf. Udall, *Apoph. of Erasm.*, 7:15; Stevenson, 780:4; Tilley, *Prov. in Eng.*, F107.

98   EVERYONE HAS HIS **FAULTS**

Cf. no. 205: Everyone makes mistakes; no. 333: No one is wise at all times

Merry Wives, I, iv, 14–15: Nobody but has his fault. ¶ *Meas. for Meas.*, V, i, 444: They say best men are moulded out of faults. ¶ *Timon*, III, i, 29: Every man has his fault. ¶ *Sonnets*, 35, 5: All men make faults.

Culman, 16: Sine vitiis nemo nascitur (No man is born without faults). ¶ *Ibid.*, 22: Nemo est hominum, in quo non aliud vitii inest (There is no man in whom there is not some fault).

Horace, *Sat.*, i, 3, 68: Vitiis nemo sine nascitur (No living wight is without faults). ¶ Seneca, *De Ira*, iii, 24, 4: Sapientissimos quoque viros multa delinquere (Even the wisest men have many faults). ¶ Erasmus, *Adagia*, 532D: Nemo vacat prorsum malo, neque crimine (No one is totally without fault, nor blame).

Cf. Tilley, *Prov. in Eng.*, M116.

99   MANY FAULTS ARE TO BE WINKED AT

Rom. & Jul., V, iii, 294–295: I, for winking at your discords . . . Have lost a brace of kinsmen. ¶ *Hen. V*, II, ii, 54–57: If little faults . . . Shall not be wink'd at, how shall we stretch our eye When capital crimes, chew'd, swallow'd, and digested, Appear before us?

Culman, 5: Crimina multa dissimulanda (Many faults are to be winked at).

Cf. Tilley, *Prov. in Eng.*, F123.

**100   WE ARE QUICK-SIGHTED TO OTHER
MEN'S FAULTS, NOT TO OUR OWN**

Lucrece, 633–634: Men's faults do seldom to themselves appear; Their own transgressions partially they smother.

Culman, 20: In aliena vitia natura sumus oculati, non in nostra (We are by nature quick-sighted to other men's faults, not to our own).

Seneca, *De Ira*, ii, 28, 8: Aliena vitia in oculis habemus, a tergo nostra sunt (The vices of others we keep before our eyes, our own behind our back).

101 THE MOST FAULTY ARE THE MOST SUSPICIOUS

3 Hen. VI, V, vi, 11: Suspicion always haunts the guilty mind. ¶ *Lucrece*, 1342–1343: But they whose guilt within their bosoms lie Imagine every eye beholds their blame.

Publilius Syrus (1835), 627: Nunquam secura est prava conscientia

(A guilty conscience never feels secure). ¶ *Ibid.*, 1103: Tuta saepe, nunquam secura, mala conscientia (An evil conscience is often quiet, but never secure).

Spenser, *Shep. Cal.*, May, 319: Πᾶς μὲν ἄπιστος ἀπιστεῖ (Who doth most mistrust is most false).

Cf. Tilley, *Prov. in Eng.*, F117.

102   BY CONSTANT **FEAR** A WISE MAN
                      ESCAPES HARM

Merry Wives, II, iii, 8–11: He is dead already if he be come. —He is wise, sir. He knew your worship would kill him if he came. ¶ *Hamlet*, V, i, 285–286: Yet have I in me something dangerous, Which let thy wisdom fear. ¶ *K. Lear*, II, iv, 308–310: A desperate train, And what they may incense him to . . . wisdom bids fear. ¶ *Cymb.*, I, iv, 146: You are afraid, and therein the wiser.

Publilius Syrus (1934), 666: Semper metuendo sapiens evitat malum (By constant fear the wise man escapes harm).

103   HE THAT LIVES ILL, **FEAR** FOLLOWS HIM

K. John, IV, ii, 56–57: Fears . . . (as they say) attend The steps of wrong.

Culman, 11: Degeneres animos timor arguit (Fear doth argue base spirits). ¶ *Ibid.*, 16: Ubi timor, ibi pudor (Where fear is, there shame is).

Erasmus, *Adagia*, 97E: Ubi timor, ibi et pudor (Where fear is, there shame is also).

Cf. Taverner, 49; Tilley, *Prov. in Eng.*, F139.

104   IN TIME OF PROSPERITY **FEAR** ADVERSITY

Timon, IV, iii, 520: You should have fear'd false times when you did feast.

Culman, 26: Rebus maxime prosperis metuenda diversa fortuna (A contrary state is to be feared, especially in prosperity).

105   IT IS FOLLY TO **FEAR** WHAT CANNOT
                     BE AVOIDED

Cf. no. 7: What cannot be altered must be borne, not blamed (lamented);
       no. 47: What cannot be cured must be endured

3 Hen. VI, V, iv, 37–38: What cannot be avoided 'Twere childish
weakness to lament or fear.

  * Publilius Syrus (1835), 924: Stultum est, timere, quod vitari non
potest (It is folly to fear what cannot be avoided).

  Seneca, *De Rem. Fortui.* (Palmer), 32–33: Stultum est timere, quod
vitare non possis (It is folly to dread what you cannot avoid).

106   WHEN THE VILLAIN (TYRANT) PRETENDS TO
                BE GOOD, IT IS TIME TO **FEAR**

Pericles, I, ii, 78: 'Tis time to fear when tyrants seem to kiss.

  * Publilius Syrus (1934), 358: Malus bonum ubi se simulat tunc est
pessimus (When the villain pretends to be good, he is most villain).

107   OFTEN WHAT YOU CANNOT **FIND**
                       COMES UNSOUGHT

All's Well, II, i, 145–147: Oft expectation fails, and most oft there
Where most it promises; and oft it hits Where hope is coldest and
despair most fits.

  Culman, 20: Insperata accidunt magis saepe, quam quae speres
(Things unlooked for do fall out oftener than what you look for).
¶*Ibid.*, 21: Multa bona multis praeter spem evenerunt (Many good
things have befel to many beyond their hopes).

108   LAY YOUR **FINGER** ON YOUR LIPS

Hamlet, I, v, 188: Your fingers on your lips, I pray. ¶*Troilus & Cres.*,
I, iii, 240: Lay thy finger on thy lips! ¶*Othello*, II, i, 223–224: Lay thy
finger thus, and let thy soul be instructed. ¶*Macb.*, I, iii, 43–45: You

seem to understand me, By each at once her choppy finger laying Upon her skinny lips.

Culman, 7: Linguam digito compesce (Keep in thy tongue with thy finger).

Juvenal, *Sat.*, ii, 160: Digito compesce labellum (Put your finger to your lip).

Cf. Tilley, *Prov. in Eng.*, F239.

109 FLATTERY IS A SIN

3 Hen. VI, V, vi, 3: 'Tis sin to flatter. ¶ *Pericles*, I, ii, 39: Flattery is the bellows blows up sin.

Publilius Syrus (1835), 1002: Vitium fuit, nunc mos est assentatio (Flattery was once a vice, now it is a fashion).

Cicero, *De Amic.*, xxiv, 89: Assentatio vitiorum adiutrix (Flattery, the handmaid of the vices).

110 THERE IS FLATTERY (FALSEHOOD) IN FRIENDSHIP

As You Like It, II, vii, 181: Most friendship is feigning. ¶ *Hen. V*, III, vii, 124–125: I will cap that proverb with 'There is flattery in friendship.' ¶ *Timon*, I, ii, 239–240: Friendship's full of dregs. Methinks false hearts should never have sound legs. ¶ *Two Noble K.*, II, ii, 228 229: But his falsehood! Why should a friend be treacherous?

Culman, 17: Adulatio, maxima in amicitia pestis (Flattery is the greatest plague in friendship).

Seneca, *Epist.*, xlv, 7: Adulatio quam similis est amicitiae (How closely flattery resembles friendship)! ¶ Tacitus, *Annals*, ii, 12: Amicis inesse adulationem (Flattery is natural in friendship).

Cf. Tilley, *Prov. in Eng.*, F41.

111 THERE IS NO FLYING WITHOUT WINGS

1 Hen. VI, I, i, 75: Another would fly swift, but wanteth wings.

Culman, 26: Sine pennis volare haud facile est (It is not an easy thing to fly without wings).

Plautus, *Poenulus*, 871: Sine pennis volare hau facilest (Flying without feathers is not easy). ¶Erasmus, *Adagia*, 847C: Sine pennis volare haud facile est (Without wings one can scarcely fly).

Cf. Smith, 212; Tilley, *Prov. in Eng.*, F407.

112   IN DUE SEASON A WISE MAN
                MAY PLAY THE **FOOL**

Cf. no. 113: No man can play the fool so well as the wise man

Twelfth N., III, i, 73–74: A wise man's art . . . folly that he wisely shows, is fit. ¶*Ant. & Cleop.*, I, i, 42–43: I'll seem the fool I am not. Antony Will be himself.

Culman, 18: Desipere in loco, summa sapientia est (It is main wisdom to play the fool in due season).

Menander, *Those Offered for Sale*, 421K: οὐ πανταχοῦ τὸ φρόνιμον ἁρμόττει παρόν, καὶ συμμανῆναι δ' ἔνια δεῖ (At times discretion should be thrown aside, and with the foolish we should play the fool). ¶Cato, *Disticha*, ii, 18: Stultitiam simulare loco, prudentia summa est (To act the fool at times is truly wise). ¶Horace, *Odes*, iv, 12, 28: Dulce est desipere in loco (It is pleasant to play the fool in the right season). ¶Erasmus, *Moriae Encomium*, 488B: Stultitiam simulare loco, sapientia summa est (To counterfeit the fool at the right time is the greatest wisdom).

Cf. J. M. Purcell, "*A. & C.*, I, i, 42–43," *Notes and Queries*, New Series, V: 5 (May 1958), 187–188; Smith, 718; Stevenson, 859: 7; Tilley, *Prov. in Eng.*, M428.

113   NO MAN CAN PLAY THE **FOOL** SO WELL AS
          THE WISE MAN

Cf. no. 112: In due season a wise man may play the fool

L. Lab. Lost, V, ii, 70–72: Folly, in wisdom hatch'd, Hath wisdom's warrant . . . And wit's own grace to grace a learned fool. ¶*Twelfth N.*, III, i, 67–68: This fellow is wise enough to play the fool, And to do that well craves a kind of wit.

Publilius Syrus (1835), 777: Qui pote consilio furere, sapere idem potest (He who can play the fool at pleasure can be wise if he will). Cf. Smith, 455; Tilley, *Prov. in Eng.*, M321.

114   FOOLS ARE WISE AS LONG AS SILENT

Merch. of V., I, i, 95–97: I do know of these That therefore only are reputed wise For saying nothing.

Publilius Syrus (1934), 693: Taciturnitas stulto homini pro sapientia est (For a fool it is wisdom to hold his tongue). ¶*Ibid.* (1835), 930: Stultus tacebit? pro sapiente habebitur (Let a fool hold his tongue, and he will pass for a sage). Cf. Tilley, *Prov. in Eng.*, F531.

115   FORTUNE DOES NOT ALWAYS SMILE

Pass. Pilgr., 20, 29: Whilst as fickle Fortune smil'd.

Culman, 14: Non semper arridet fortuna (Fortune does not always smile).

116   FORTUNE IS FICKLE

1 Hen. VI, V, iii, 134: Fortune's fickleness. ¶*Rom. & Jul.*, III, v, 60: Fortune, Fortune! all men call thee fickle. ¶*Pass. Pilgr.*, 17, 15: O frowning Fortune, cursed fickle dame! ¶*Ibid.*, 20, 29: Fickle Fortune. ¶*Hen. V*, III, vi, 29: Giddy Fortune's furious fickle wheel.

* Publilius Syrus (1934), 335: Levis est Fortuna: cito reposcit quod dedit (Fickle is fortune: she soon demands back what she gave).

Ovid, *Tristia*, v, 8, 15–18: Passibus ambiguis Fortuna volubilis errat ... et tantum constans in levitate sua est (Changeable fortune wanders abroad with aimless steps, steadfast only in its own fickleness). ¶Seneca, *Medea*, 219: Rapida fortuna ac levis (Swift and fickle is fortune). ¶Seneca, *Epist.*, xiii, 11: Habet etiam mala fortuna levitatem (Even bad fortune is fickle). Cf. Tilley, *Prov. in Eng.*, F606.

**117   FORTUNE MAKES A FOOL OF HIM
WHOM SHE FAVORS TOO MUCH**

As You Like It, II, vii, 18–19: 'Good morrow, fool,' quoth I. 'No, sir,'
quoth he, 'Call me not fool till heaven hath sent me fortune.'

* Publilius Syrus (1934), 203: Fortuna nimium quem fovet stultum
facit (Fortune turns her spoiled darling into a fool).

Seneca, *Ad Helviam de Con.*, v, 4: Neminem adversa fortuna comminuit, nisi quem secunda decepit (No one is crushed by hostile fortune
who is not first deceived by its smiles).

Cf. Malone, *Variorum* (1821), VI, 401; Baldwin, I, 603–604; Tilley,
Prov. in Eng., G220.

**118   A MEAN FORTUNE IS SAFER THAN
A LOFTY FORTUNE**

3 Hen. VI, IV, vi, 19–20: I may conquer fortune's spite By living low,
where fortune cannot hurt me.

Culman, 20: Humilis fortuna tutior est quam excelsa (A mean fortune
is more safe than a lofty).

**119   ILL FORTUNE IS TO BE OVERCOME
BY SUFFERING**

Ant. & Cleop., IV, xiv, 135–138: Do not please sharp fate To grace it
with your sorrows. Bid that welcome Which comes to punish us, and
we punish it, Seeming to bear it lightly.

Culman, 26: Superanda omnis fortuna ferendo est (All fortune is to
be overcome by suffering).

Vergil, *Aeneid*, v, 710: Superanda omnis fortuna ferendo est (All
fortune is to be overcome by bearing). ¶Erasmus, *Adagia*, 818E: In
re mala, animo si bono utare, adjuvat (In difficulty, if you use a pleasant
mind, it will help).

Cf. Tilley, *Prov. in Eng.*, E136.

120 IN ALL HUMAN AFFAIRS FORTUNE (PROVIDENCE) RULES

Cf. no. 66: The doom of destiny cannot be avoided

Rom. & Jul., V, iii, 153–154: A greater power than we can contradict Hath thwarted our intents. ¶ *Merch. of V.*, II, i, 15–16: The lott'ry of my destiny Bars me the right of voluntary choosing. ¶ *Jul. Caesar*, V, i, 104–107: To prevent The time of life—arming myself with patience To stay the providence of some high powers That govern us below. ¶ *Hamlet*, III, ii, 221–222: Our wills and fates do so contrary run That our devices still are overthrown. ¶ *Ibid.*, V, ii, 10–11: There's a divinity that shapes our ends, Rough-hew them how we will. ¶ *K. Lear*, IV, iii, 34–35: It is the stars, The stars above us, govern our conditions. ¶ *Pericles*, II, iii, 12: 'Tis more by fortune, lady, than my merit. ¶ *Tempest*, V, i, 256–258: Let no man take care for himself; for all is but fortune.

Culman, 31: Eveniunt non quae nos instituimus, sed quae Deus decrevit (Those things befall not, which we determine, but which God hath decreed). ¶ Publilius Syrus (1934), 222: Fortuna plus homini quam consilium valet (Luck avails a man more than policy). ¶ *Ibid.* (1835), 999: Vitam regit fortuna, non sapientia (Fortune is mistress of life, and not wisdom).

Sophocles, *Philoctetes*, 1316–1317: ἀνθρώποισι τὰς μὲν ἐκ θεῶν τύχας δοθείσας ἔστ' ἀναγκαῖον φέρειν (What fates the gods allot to men they needs must bear). ¶ Euripides, *Hecuba*, 491: τύχην δὲ πάντα τἀν βροτοῖς ἐπισκοπεῖν (Chance controls all things among men). ¶ Plautus, *Captivi*, 304: Fortuna humana fingit artatque ut lubet (Fortune molds us, pinches us, to suit her whims). ¶ Cicero, *Tusc. Disp.*, v, 9, 25: Vitam regit fortuna, non sapientia (Fortune, not wisdom, rules the life of men). ¶ Ovid, *Ex Ponto*, iv, 3, 49: Ludit in humanis divina potentia rebus (Divine power plays with human affairs); cf. *Metam.*, viii, 619. ¶ Seneca, *Hippolytus*, 978–979: Res humanas ordine nullo Fortuna regit (Fortune without order rules the affairs of men). ¶ Seneca, *Octavia*, 924: Regitur fatis mortale genus (Our mortal race is ruled by fate). ¶ Statius, *Thebaidos*, vii, 197–198: Immoto deducimur orbe fatorum (It is fate's unchanging wheel that ordains our destiny).

121   WHEN **FORTUNE** IS AGAINST US,
                   WE HAVE NO FRIENDS

Cf. no. 127: Our friends with our fortunes change

Pass. Pilgr., 20, 47–50: If Fortune once do frown, Then farewell his great renown! They that fawn'd on him before Use his company no more. ¶*Troilus & Cres.*, III, iii, 75–76: Greatness, once fall'n out with fortune, Must fall out with men too.

Culman, 18: Qui fortuna adversatur, amicos non habet (He hath no friends whom fortune is against). ¶*Ibid.*: Diligitur nemo, nisi cui fortuna secunda est (No man is beloved but he to whom fortune is favourable). ¶Publilius Syrus (1835), 279: Fortuna quo se, eodem et inclinat favor (When fortune is on our side, popular favor bears her company).

Ovid, *Ex Ponto*, ii, 3, 23: Diligitur nemo, nisi cui fortuna secunda est (There is love for none except him whom fortune favors). ¶Ovid, *Tristia*, i, 9, 10: Nullus ad amissas ibit amicus opes (No friend will approach when wealth is lost). ¶Erasmus, *Adagia*, 658F: Viri infortunati procul amici (The friends of an unfortunate man are far away).

Cf. Stevenson, 905:5.

122   MOST **FOUL**, MOST FAIR

Much Ado, IV, i, 104: Most foul, most fair! ¶*Macb.*, I, i, 10: Fair is foul, and foul is fair. ¶*Ibid.*, iii, 38: So foul and fair a day I have not seen.

* Publilius Syrus (1835), 309: Graviu'st malum comi quod aspectu latet (The worst evil is that which is hidden under a pleasing exterior).

Cf. Tilley, *Prov. in Eng.*, F29.

123   A **FRIEND** SHOULD BEAR A
                   FRIEND'S INFIRMITIES

Jul. Caesar, IV, iii, 86: A friend should bear his friend's infirmities.

Publilius Syrus (1934), 522: Peccatum amici veluti tuum recte putes (You would do right to consider your friend's fault as if it were your own).

Plautus, *Captivi*, 151: Laudo, malum cum amici tuom ducis malum (I appreciate this, that you consider your friend's disaster your own).

124 A TRUE **FRIEND** IS A GREAT TREASURE

Timon, II, ii, 192–193: You Mistake my fortunes; I am wealthy in my friends.

Culman, 13: Ingens thesaurus, bonus amicus (A good friend is a great treasure). ¶ *Ibid.*, 16: Ubi amici, ibi opes (Where friends are, there riches are). ¶ *Ibid.*, 17: Amicus verus, thesaurus est magnus (A true friend is a great treasury). ¶ Publilius Syrus (1934), 53: Amico firmo nihil emi melius potest (There's nothing better in the market than a staunch friend).

Euripides, *Orestes*, 1155: οὐκ ἔστιν οὐδὲν κρεῖσσον ἢ φίλος σαφής (Nothing is better than a loyal friend). ¶ Xenophon, *Memorabilia*, ii, 4, 1: πάντων κτημάτων κράτιστον εἴη φίλος σαφὴς καὶ ἀγαθός (Of all possessions, the most precious is a good and sincere friend). ¶ Plautus, *Truculentus*, 885: Verum est verbum quod memoratur: ubi amici ibidem sunt opes (True is the proverb they quote: "Where your friends are, there your riches are"). ¶ Erasmus, *Adagia*, 121E: Ubi amici, ibi opes (Where friends are, there riches are).

Cf. Udall, *Apoph. of Erasm.*, 6:13; 14:31; Taverner, 14; Stevenson, 893:5; 898:6; Tilley, *Prov. in Eng.*, F719.

125 AMONG **FRIENDS** ALL THINGS ARE COMMON

Timon, I, ii, 105–109: What better or properer can we call our own than the riches of our friends? O, what a precious comfort 'tis to have so many like brothers commanding one another's fortunes!

Publilius Syrus (1835), 1051: Minime amicus sum, fortunae particeps nisi tuae (I am not your friend unless I share in your fortunes).

Euripides, *Andromache*, 376–377: φίλων γὰρ οὐδὲν ἴδιον οἵτινες φίλοι ὀρθῶς πεφύκασ, ἀλλὰ κοινὰ χρήματα (For nothing that friends have, if true friends they be, is private; held in common is all wealth). ¶ Aristotle, *Politics*, ii, 2, 5: κατὰ τὴν παροιμίαν κοινὰ τὰ φίλων (Friends'

goods common goods, as the proverb says); cf. *N. Ethics*, viii, 9, 1.
¶Terence, *Adelphoe*, 803–804: Vetus verbum hoc quidemst, communia esse amicorum inter se omnia (It's an old saying that friends have all things in common). ¶Cicero, *De Offic.*, i, 16, 51: In Graecorum proverbio est, amicorum esse communia omnia (In the light indicated by the Greek proverb: "Amongst friends all things in common"). ¶Seneca, *De Benef.*, vii, 12, 5: Quidquid habet amicus, commune est nobis (Whatever our friend possesses is common to us). ¶Erasmus, *Adagia*, 13F: Amicorum communia sunt omnia (Among friends all things are common).

Cf. Taverner, 65; Bacon, *Promus*, 984; Stevenson, 903:1–4; Tilley, *Prov. in Eng.*, F729; Charles G. Smith, *Spenser's Theory of Friendship* (1935), 50–52.

126   FAITHFUL **FRIENDS** ARE HARD TO FIND

Pass. Pilgr., 20, 34: Faithful friends are hard to find.

Culman, 10: Amici boni rari sunt (Good friends are rare).

Plautus, *Trinummus*, 620: Nimium difficilest reperiri amicum ita ut nomen cluet (How hard it is to find a friend that lives up to the name). ¶Plutarch, *Moralia*: *On Having Many Friends*, 97B: σπάνιον καὶ δυσεύρετόν ἐστι φίλος βέβαιος (A steadfast friend is something rare and hard to find).

Cf. Stevenson, 898:4.

127 OUR **FRIENDS** WITH OUR FORTUNES CHANGE

Cf. no. 121: When fortune is against us, we have no friends

Hamlet, III, ii, 210–211: 'Tis not strange That even our loves should with our fortunes change.

Culman, 11: Cum fortuna mutantur amici (Friends are changed with fortune).

Plautus, *Stichus*, 520–522: Ut cuique homini res paratast, perinde

amicis utitur: si res firma, item firmi amici sunt; sin res laxe labat, itidem amici conlabascunt: res amicos invenit (On anyone's financial standing hangs his status with his friends: if he is in a sound financial state, his friends are sound; but once that state begins wavering wildly, his friends co-waver likewise: friends are matters of finance).
Cf. Stevenson, 905:5.

128 WE SHOULD MAKE USE OF OUR **FRIENDS**

Timon, I, ii, 98–101: What need we have any friends if we should ne'er have need of 'em? They were the most needless creatures living, should we ne'er have use for 'em.

Culman, 1: Amicis utere (Make use of thy friends). ¶Publilius Syrus (1835), 974: Utendum amicis, tum, quum eorum copia est (We should use our friends while we have plenty of them).

129 **FRIENDSHIP** IS BASED ON EQUALITY

Hen. VIII, II, iv, 17–18: More assurance Of equal friendship.

Publilius Syrus (1835), 32: Amicitia pares aut accipit, aut facit (Friendship either finds or makes equals).

Euripides, *Phoenissae*, 536–538: Ἰσότητα τιμᾶν, ἣ φίλους ἀεὶ φίλοις ... συνδεῖ (Equality, which knitteth friends to friends). ¶Plato, *Laws*, vi, 757A: παλαιὸς γὰρ λόγος ἀληθὴς ὤν, ὡς ἰσότης φιλότητα ἀπεργάζεται (There is an old and true saying that equality produces amity). ¶Aristotle, *N. Ethics*, viii, 5, 5: λέγεται γὰρ φιλότης ἡ ἰσότης (For there is a saying, "Friendship is equality"). ¶Aristotle, *Politics*, iii, 11, 9: ὅ γε φίλος ἴσος καὶ ὅμοιος (A friend is one's equal and like). ¶Diogenes Laertius, *Pythagoras*, viii, 10: φιλίαν ἰσότητα (Friendship is equality). ¶Erasmus, *Adagia*, 14F: Amicitia aequalitas (Friendship is based on equality).

Cf. Taverner, 66; Tilley, *Eliz. Prov. Lore*, 278, *Prov. in Eng.*, F761; Charles G. Smith, *Spenser's Theory of Friendship* (1935), 31–33.

130   **FRIENDSHIP** IS TO BE PREFERRED
BEFORE ALL THINGS

L. Lab. Lost, IV, ii, 167–168: Society (saith the text) is the happiness of
life.

Culman, 10: Amicitia omnibus rebus anteponenda (Friendship is to
be preferred before all things). ¶ *Ibid.*, 14: Nulla amicorum melior
possessio (No possession is better than that of friends).

Cf. Baldwin, I, 592.

131   TRUE **FRIENDSHIP** (LOVE) IS ETERNAL

Sonnets, 116, 2–3: Love is not love Which alters when it alteration
finds. ¶ *Two Noble K.*, II, ii, 114–117: I do not think it possible our
friendship Should ever leave us. —Till our deaths it cannot, And after
death our spirits shall . . . love eternally.

Publilius Syrus (1835), 734: Quae desiit amicitia, ne coepit quidem
(The friendship that can come to an end never really began).

Aristotle, *N. Ethics*, ix, 1, 3: ἡ [friendship] δὲ τῶν ἠθῶν καθ᾽ αὑτὴν
οὖσα μένει (Friendship based on character is disinterested, and therefore
lasting). ¶ Cicero, *De Amic.*, ix, 32: Verae amicitiae sempiternae sunt
(Real friendships are eternal).

Cf. Tilley, *Prov. in Eng.*, L539.

132   ONE MAN'S **GAIN** IS ANOTHER MAN'S LOSS

Cf. no. 256: The rising of one man is the falling of another

2 Hen. VI, IV, x, 22: I seek not to wax great by others' waning. ¶ *Macb.*,
I, ii, 67: What he hath lost noble Macbeth hath won.

* Publilius Syrus (1934), 337: Lucrum sine damno alterius fieri non
potest (Gain cannot be made without another's loss).

Seneca, *De Ira*, ii, 8, 2: Nulli nisi ex alterius iniuria quaestus est (No
one makes gain save by another's loss).

Cf. Tilley, *Eliz. Prov. Lore*, 738, *Prov. in Eng.*, M337.

133   A **GIFT** IS VALUED BY THE MIND
OF THE GIVER

Hamlet, III, i, 100–101: To the noble mind Rich gifts wax poor when givers prove unkind.

Culman, 11: Beneficium animo donantis metiendum (A benefit is to be measured by the mind of the giver). ❡*Ibid.*, 12: Donum a dantis animo pensatur (A gift is valued by the mind of the giver).

Seneca, *De Benef.*, i, 6, 1: Beneficium non in eo, quod fit aut datur, consistit, sed in ipso dantis aut facientis animo (A benefit consists, not in what is done or given, but in the mind of the giver or doer). ❡Erasmus, *Adagia*, 614C: Munerum animus optimus ... quo significatur, in amicorum muneribus non esse spectandum rei missae precium, sed mittentis potius animum (With a gift the good will is most important, and what makes a gift valuable is not its intrinsic value but the good will and intention of the giver).

Cf. Taverner, 25; Tilley, *Eliz. Prov. Lore*, 732, *Prov. in Eng.*, G97.

134   THE GIVER OF A **GIFT** DESERVED
IS REWARDED

Timon, I, i, 288–291: No meed but he repays Sevenfold above itself. No gift to him But breeds the giver a return exceeding All use of quittance.

* Publilius Syrus (1934), 68: Beneficium dando accipit qui digno dedit (The giver of a gift deserved gets benefit by giving). ❡*Ibid.*, 541: Probo beneficium qui dat ex parte accipit (The giver of a benefit to the good is in part the receiver). ❡*Ibid.*, 582: Quicquid bono concedas, des partem tibi (Whatever you may grant to the good, you give partly to yourself).

Cf. Tilley, *Prov. in Eng.*, G128.

135   **GIFTS** OFTEN CATCH MEN

Two Gent., III, i, 89–91: Win her with gifts, if she respect not words. Dumb jewels often in their silent kind More than quick words do move a woman's mind. ❡*Hamlet*, I, v, 43–45: Traitorous gifts ... gifts, that have the power So to seduce!

Culman, 7: Munera capiunt homines (Gifts do catch men).
Cf. Tilley, *Prov. in Eng.*, W704.

136   IT IS BETTER TO **GIVE**
          THAN TO TAKE (RECEIVE)

Timon, I, ii, 10–11: I gave it freely ever; and there's none Can truly say
he gives, if he receives.

Publilius Syrus (1835), 706: Praestare cuncta pulchrum est, exigere
nihil (To give everything and not demand anything in return, that is
beautiful).

Cf. Tilley, *Prov. in Eng.*, G119.

137   **GOD** RULES ALL THINGS

Cf. no. 138: All things are in the hand of God

Rich. II, III, iii, 17–19: The heavens are over our heads. —I know it,
uncle, and oppose not myself Against their will. ¶ *Troilus & Cres.*, I, ii,
83–84: Well, the gods are above; time must friend or end. ¶ *Othello*, II,
iii, 105–107: Well, God's above all; and there be souls must be saved,
and there be souls must not be saved. ¶ *Hen. VIII*, III, i, 100–101:
Heaven is above all yet. There sits a judge That no king can corrupt.

Culman, 29: Consilio Dei, omnia fiunt (All things are done by God's
decree). ¶ *Ibid.*, 31: Deus regit omnia (God ruleth all things).

Homer, *Iliad*, xix, 90: θεὸς διὰ πάντα τελευτᾷ (It is God that brings
all things to their issue). ¶ Seneca, *Epist.*, cvii, 9: Optimum est . . . deum,
quo auctore cuncta proveniunt, sine murmuratione comitari (It is best
to attend uncomplainingly upon God under whose guidance everything
comes to pass).

Cf. Stevenson, 982: 5–8; Tilley, *Prov. in Eng.*, H348.

138   ALL THINGS ARE IN THE HAND OF **GOD**

Cf. no. 137: God rules all things

Hen. V, III, vi, 178: We are in God's hand. ¶ *Merry Wives*, I, iv, 154:
All is in his hands above. ¶ *Macb.*, II, iii, 136: In the great hand of God
I stand.

Culman, 34: Omnia nostra in manu Dei posita (All our things are in the hands of God).

139   HELP IS TO BE EXPECTED FROM **GOD**

2 Hen. VI, IV, iv, 55: God, our hope, will succour us. ¶ *1 Hen. IV*, V, i, 120: And God befriend us as our cause is just!

Culman, 29: Auxilium a Domino expectandum (Help is to be expected from God).

140   HELP THYSELF ∧ND **GOD** WILL HELP THEE

Rich. II, III, ii, 29–30: The means that heaven yields must be embrac'd, And not neglected.

Culman, 6: Industrium adjuvat Deus (God helps the painful person).

Aeschylus, *Frag.*, 223: φιλεῖ δὲ τῷ κάμνοντι συσπεύδειν θεός (God loves to help him who tries to help himself). ¶ Erasmus, *Adagia*, 929C: Industriam adjuvat Deus (God helps the industrious).

Cf. Taverner, 54; Stevenson, 979 : 4; Tilley, *Prov. in Eng.*, G236.

141   **GOLD** OFTEN CORRUPTS MEN'S SOULS

Rom. & Jul., I, i, 221: Saint-seducing gold. ¶ *Ibid.*, V, i, 80–82: Gold— worse poison to men's souls, Doing more murther in this loathsome world, Than these poor compounds that thou mayst not sell. ¶ *Rich. III*, IV, ii, 34–35: Know'st thou not any whom corrupting gold Will tempt unto a close exploit of death?

Culman, 17: Aurum multis saepe suasit perperam (Gold hath ofttimes persuaded men amiss).

Plautus, *Captivi*, 328: Odi ego aurum: multa multis saepe suasit perperam (Gold! I despise it: it has led many a man into many a wrong course).

Cf. Stevenson, 989 : 8; 990 : 2.

142 WHEN **GOLD** ARGUES THE CAUSE, ELOQUENCE IS IMPOTENT

Cf. no. 209: Money masters all things

Rich. III, IV, ii, 38: Gold were as good as twenty orators.

Publilius Syrus (1835), 66: Auro suadente nil potest oratio (When gold argues the cause, eloquence is impotent).

Erasmus, *Adagia*, 786D: Auro loquente, nihil pollet quaevis oratio (When gold speaks, eloquence is of no value whatever). ¶ Barnfield, *Aff. Shep.* (Percy S.), 48: Gold is a deepe-perswading orator.

Cf. Stevenson, 988 : 8.

143 SET **GOOD** AGAINST EVIL (DO GOOD FOR EVIL)

Rich. III, I, ii, 68–69: Lady, you know no rules of charity, Which renders good for bad, blessings for curses. ¶ *Ibid.*, iii, 335: God bids us do good for evil. ¶ *All's Well*, II, v, 53: But we must do good against evil.

Culman, 34: Malum non alio malo, sed bono pellitur (Evil is not put away by another evil, but by good).

Cf. Tilley, *Prov. in Eng.*, G318.

144 MUTE **GRIEF** FEELS A KEENER PANG THAN THAT WHICH CRIES ALOUD

Cf. no. 227: Pain (Grief, Love) that has no voice amid torture is a hell; no. 277: Speech is a cure for sorrow

3 Hen. VI, II, i, 85: To weep is to make less the depth of grief.

Publilius Syrus (1835), 671: Pejora querulo cogitat mutus dolor (Mute grief feels a keener pang than that which cries aloud).

Ovid, *Tristia*, v, 1, 59: Est aliquid, fatale malum per verba levare (It is something to lighten with words a fated evil). ¶ Seneca, *Troades*, 765: Fletus aerumnas levat (Weeping lightens woe). ¶ Seneca, *Epist.*, xcix, 15: Excidunt etiam retinentibus lacrimae et animum profusae levant (Tears fall, no matter how we try to check them, and by being shed they ease the soul).

145   TO SPARE THE **GUILTY** IS TO INJURE
THE INNOCENT

Cf. no. 172: Too much lenity encourages wrongdoing; no. 229: Pardon
makes offenders

Meas. for Meas., II, ii, 99–102: Yet show some pity. —I show it most of
all when I show justice; For then I pity those I do not know, Which a
dismiss'd offence would after gall.

* Publilius Syrus (1835), 116: Bonis nocet, quisquis pepercerit malis
(To spare the guilty is to injure the innocent).
Cf. Tilley, *Prov. in Eng.*, E200.

146   **HARES** MAY PULL DEAD LIONS
BY THE BEARD

K. John, II, i, 137–138: You are the hare of whom the proverb goes,
Whose valour plucks dead lions by the beard.

Publilius Syrus (1835), 428: Leo a leporibus insultatur mortuus
(Hares can gambol over the body of a dead lion).

Erasmus, *Adagia*, 1118A: Mortuo leoni et lepores insultant (Hares
taunt the dead lion).

Cf. Tilley, *Eliz. Prov. Lore*, 322, *Prov. in Eng.*, H165.

147 TO BE ABLE TO DO **HARM** AND TO ABSTAIN
FROM DOING IT IS NOBLE

Cf. no. 34: Be able to conquer your enemy, but spare him

L. Lab. Lost, II, i, 56–58: The young Dumain, a well-accomplish'd
youth, Of all that virtue love for virtue lov'd; Most power to do most
harm, least knowing ill. ¶ *As You Like It*, IV, iii, 129–131: But kindness,
nobler ever than revenge . . . Made him give battle to the lioness.
¶ *Meas. for Meas.*, II, ii, 107–109: It is excellent To have a giant's
strength; but it is tyrannous To use it like a giant. ¶ *Coriol.*, V, i, 18–19:
I minded him how royal 'twas to pardon When it was less expected.
¶ *Sonnets*, 94, 1–5: They that have pow'r to hurt and will do none . . .

They rightly do inherit heaven's graces. ¶*Cymb.*, V, v, 417–419: Kneel not to me. The pow'r that I have on you is to spare you; The malice towards you to forgive you. ¶*Tempest*, V, i, 27–28: The rarer action is In virtue than in vengeance.

Publilius Syrus (1934), 442: Nocere posse et nolle laus amplissima est (Power to harm without the will is the most ample fame).

Ovid, *Heroides*, xii, 75–76: Perdere posse sat est, siquem iuvet ipsa potestas; sed tibi servatus gloria maior ero (To have power to ruin is enough, if anyone delight in power for itself; but to save me will be greater glory).

Cf. Tilley, *Eliz. Prov. Lore*, 69, *Prov. in Eng.*, H170.

148   **HASTE** BREEDS ERROR

Cf. no. 149: The more the haste, the less the speed

L. Lab. Lost, II, i, 238–239: His tongue, all impatient to speak and not see, Did stumble with haste. ¶*Rom. & Jul.*, II, iii, 93–94: O, let us hence! I stand on sudden haste. —Wisely, and slow. They stumble that run fast.

Culman, 19: Festinationis comites sunt error & poenitentia (Errour and repentance are the campanions of haste). ¶*Ibid.*, 23: Omnis res properando parit errorem (Everything breeds errour by making haste). ¶Publilius Syrus (1835), 1029: Festinationis error comes et poenitentia (Error and repentance are the attendants on hasty decisions).

149 THE MORE THE **HASTE**, THE LESS THE SPEED

Cf. no. 148: Haste breeds error

Venus & A., 909: Her more than haste is mated with delays. ¶*Rom. & Jul.*, II, vi, 15: Too swift arrives as tardy as too slow.

Culman, 25: Qui nimium properat, serius absolvit (He finishes too late who goes too fast). ¶Publilius Syrus (1835), 782: Qui properat nimium, res absolvit serius (He gets through too late who goes too fast).

Erasmus, *Adagia*, 842A: Qui nimium properat, serius absolvit (He finishes too late who goes too fast).

Cf. Tilley, *Prov. in Eng.*, H198.

150   NOTHING IS BETTER IN THIS LIFE
                      THAN **HEALTH**

Rich. II, II, i, 91–93: O, no! thou diest, though I the sicker be. —I am
in health, I breathe, and see thee ill. —Now, he that made me knows I
see thee ill. ¶ *2 Hen. IV*, II, ii, 110–113: How doth . . . your master?
—In bodily health, sir. —Marry, the immortal part needs a physician.
¶ *Winter's T.*, I, ii, 304–306: Were my wive's liver Infected as her life,
she would not live The running of one glass.

Culman, 16: Sanitate nihil in vita melius (Nothing is better in this
life than health).

Cf. Tilley, *Prov. in Eng.*, H285.

151   A **HESITANT** MIND IS THE
                   HANDMAID OF WISDOM

Troilus & Cres., II, ii, 15–16: Modest doubt is call'd The beacon of the
wise. ¶ *Macb.*, IV, iii, 119–120: Modest wisdom plucks me From over-
credulous haste.

Publilius Syrus (1934), 320: Incertus animus dimidium est sapientiae
(The hesitant mind is the half of wisdom).

Sidney, *Arcadia* (Feuillerat), I, 178: The handmaid of wisdome is
slow belief. ¶ Spenser, *F. Q.*, IV, iii, 41, 9: Some that would seeme
wise, their wonder turnd to dout.

152   THE **HIGHER** THE STANDING,
                   THE GREATER THE FALL

Rich. III, I, iii, 259–260: They that stand high . . . if they fall, they dash
themselves to pieces.

* Publilius Syrus (1934), 189: Excelsis multo facilius casus nocet
(The exalted are much more readily hurt by misfortune).

Cf. Tilley, *Prov. in Eng.*, S823.

153   HONOR IS STAINED WHEN YOU SEEK
IT FOR THE UNWORTHY

Timon, I, i, 15–17: When we for recompense have prais'd the vile, It stains the glory in that happy verse Which aptly sings the good.

Publilius Syrus (1934), 268: Honestum laedis cum pro indigno intervenis (You hurt the honorable by intervening for the unworthy).

¶ *Ibid*. (1835), 332: Honestatem laedes, quum pro indigno petes (You stain honor when you seek it for an unworthy man).

154   NO ONE EVER LOST HIS HONOR SAVE
HIM WHO HAD IT NOT

1 Hen. VI, IV, v, 40: Thou never hadst renown, nor canst not lose it.

¶ *As You Like It*, I, ii, 81–83: But if you swear by that that is not, you are not forsworn. No more was this knight, swearing by his honour, for he never had any.

* Publilius Syrus (1934), 212: Fidem nemo umquam perdit nisi qui non habet (None ever loses honor save him who has it not).

Cf. Tilley, *Prov. in Eng.*, M326.

155   HOPE IS THE ONLY MEDICINE FOR
THE MISERABLE

Meas. for Meas., III, i, 2–3: The miserable have no other medicine But only hope.

Culman, 9: Spes servat afflictos (Hope preserves the afflicted).

Erasmus, *Adagia*, 1039C: Spes servat afflictos (Hope supports the afflicted).

Cf. Tilley, *Prov. in Eng.*, H602.

156   HUNGER IS THE BEST SAUCE

Two Noble K., III, iii, 24–25: How tastes your victuals? Your hunger needs no sauce, I see.

Culman, 5: Fames optimus coquus (Hunger is the best sauce).

Cato, *Collectio Monos.*, 39: Condit fercla fames (Hunger is sauce).
¶Cicero, *De Fin.*, ii, 28, 90: Cibi condimentum esse famem (The best sauce for food is hunger). ¶Erasmus, *Adagia*, 630D: Optimum condimentum fames (Hunger is the best sauce).
Cf. Udall, *Apoph. of Erasm.*, 2:6; 14:30; Tilley, *Prov. in Eng.*, H819.

157   IDLENESS IS THE NURSE OF EVIL

Ant. & Cleop., I, ii, 133–134: Ten thousand harms more than the ills I know My idleness doth hatch.
Culman, 12: Ex otio vitia proveniunt (Vices come from idleness).
¶*Ibid.*, 14: Otium multa docet vitia (Idleness doth teach many vices).
¶*Ibid.*, 22: Multa mala affert hominibus otium (Idleness doth occasion many mischiefs to men). ¶*Ibid.*, 25: Quam multa mala hominibus affert otium (How many mischiefs doth idleness bring upon men)? ¶Publilius Syrus (1835), 321: Homines nihil agendo agere consuescunt male (By doing nothing, men learn to do ill).
Cf. Udall, *Apoph. of Erasm.*, 10:21; Tilley, *Prov. in Eng.*, I13.

158   INGRATITUDE IS THE WORST OF ALL VICES

Twelfth N., III, iv, 388–390: I hate ingratitude more ... Than , , , any taint of vice.
Culman, 13: Ingratitudo vitiorum omnium caput (Unthankfulness is the head of all vices). ¶*Ibid.*, 34: Nihil pejus ingratitudine (Nothing is worse than ingratitude).
Cf. Tilley, *Prov. in Eng.*, I66.

159   INJURIES (BURDENS, WOES) SLIGHTED
BECOME NONE AT ALL

Rich. II, I, iii, 280–281: Woe doth the heavier sit Where it perceives it is but faintly borne. ¶*Ibid.*, 292–293: For gnarling sorrow hath less power to bite The man that mocks at it and sets it light.

Culman, 21: Leve fit, quod bene fertur onus (The burden that is borne well is made light).
Cf. Tilley, *Prov. in Eng.*, I72.

160 THERE IS NO JOY WITHOUT SORROW

Hamlet, III, ii, 208–209: Where joy most revels, grief doth most lament; Grief joys, joy grieves, on slender accident. ¶ *Twelfth N.*, II, iv, 71–73: I'll pay thy pleasure then. —Truly, sir, and pleasure will be paid one time or another.

Culman, 6: Gaudium dolori junctum (Joy is joined to grief).

Erasmus, *Adagia*, 943A: Gaudium dolori junctum (Joy is joined to grief).

Cf. Tilley, *Prov. in Eng.*, P420.

161 BEFORE WE JUDGE, WE SHOULD HEAR ALL PARTS

Hamlet, I, iii, 68–69: Give every man thine ear, but few thy voice; Take each man's censure, but reserve thy judgment.

Culman, 33: Judicandum est post causam cognitam (We must judge after the cause be known). ¶ * Publilius Syrus (1835), 189: Deliberandum est diu, quod statuendum est semel (What is to be once resolved on should be first often well considered).

Aristophanes, *The Wasps*, 725: πρὶν ἂν ἀμφοῖν μῦθον ἀκούσῃς, οὐκ ἂν δικάσαις (Don't make up your mind until you have heard both sides).

Cf. Stevenson, 1281:14; Tilley, *Prov. in Eng.*, M299.

162 NO ONE SHOULD BE JUDGE IN HIS OWN CAUSE

Venus & A., 220: Being judge in love, she cannot right her cause. ¶ *Merch. of V.*, II, ix, 61–62: To offend and judge are distinct offices And of opposed natures. ¶ *Twelfth N.*, V, i, 362–363: Thou shalt be

both the plaintiff and the judge Of thine own cause. ¶ *Meas. for Meas.*,
V, i, 166–167: Be you judge Of your own cause.
    Publilius Syrus (1835), 555: Nemo esse judex in sua causa potest (No
one should judge in his own cause).
    Cf. Tilley, *Prov. in Eng.*, M341.

163   DEFECT OF **JUDGMENT** IS OFTEN
                THE CAUSE OF FEAR

Cymb., IV, ii, 111–112: Defect of judgment Is oft the cause of fear.
    Culman, 27: Semper metuit nimium praesaga mens (A mind that
guesseth too much aforehand, doth always fear).

164   IT IS BARBAROUS TO **KILL** A CHILD

Rich. III, I, iii, 183–184: 'Twas the foulest deed to slay that babe And
the most merciless that e'er was heard of!
    Publilius Syrus (1934), 123: Crudelis est non fortis qui infantem
necat (Barbarous, not brave, is he who kills a child).

165   **KINDNESS** (GENTLENESS) CAN WIN
                WHAT FORCE CANNOT

As You Like It, II, vii, 102–103: Your gentleness shall force More than
your force move us to gentleness. ¶ *Pericles*, II, ii, 27: The motto thus
in Spanish, 'Piu por dulzura que por fuerza.'
    Publilius Syrus (1934), 718: Virtute quod non possis blanditia auferas
(Kindness can win what force cannot).

166   BE **KIND-SPOKEN**

Rich. II, III, ii, 193: Speak sweetly, man, although thy looks be sour.
    Culman, 1: Blandus esto (Be kind-spoken).

167   **KNOW** THYSELF

Venus & A., 525 : Before I know myself, seek not to know me. ❡*Merch. of V.*, I, i, 7 : I have much ado to know myself. ❡*As You Like It*, III, v, 57 : Know yourself. ❡*Hamlet*, V, ii, 146–147 : To know a man well were to know himself. ❡*All's Well*, V, iii, 105–106 : If you know That you are well acquainted with yourself. ❡*Meas. for Meas.*, III, ii, 246–247 : One that . . . contended especially to know himself. ❡*K. Lear*, I, i, 296–297 : He hath ever but slenderly known himself. ❡*Ibid.*, iv, 272– 273 : Men . . . Which know themselves. ❡*Macb.*, IV, ii, 18–19 : When we . . . do not know ourselves. ❡*Coriol.*, II, i, 75–76 : You know neither me, yourselves, nor anything. ❡*Hen. VIII*, II, ii, 23 : He'll never know himself.

Culman, 1 : Cognosce teipsum (Know thy selfe).

Aristotle, *Rhet.*, ii, 21, 13 : Γνῶθι σαυτόν (Know thyself). ❡Cicero, *Tusc. Disp.*, i, 22, 52 : Cum igitur *Nosce te*, dicit, hoc dicit: *Nosce animum tuum* (When, therefore, he [Apollo] says, "Know thyself," he says, "Know thy soul"). ❡Seneca, *Epist.*, xciv, 28 : Te nosce (Know thyself). ❡Juvenal, *Sat.*, xi, 27 : E caelo descendit γνῶθι σεαυτόν ("Know thyself" descended from heaven). ❡Erasmus, *Adagia*, 258D: Nosce teipsum (Know thyself).

Cf. Taverner, 19; Bacon, *Promus*, 1397; Stevenson, 2066:4; Tilley, *Prov. in Eng.*, K175.

168   ON EARTH NOTHING **LASTS** FOREVER

All's Well, II, ii, 60–61 : Things may serve long, but not serve ever.

Culman, 2 : Nihil diuturnum (Nothing is long-lasting).

Seneca, *Ad Polybium de Con.*, i, 1 : Nihil perpetuum (Nothing is everlasting).

Cf. Tilley, *Prov. in Eng.*, G58.

169   BETTER **LATE** THAN NEVER

T. of Shrew, V, i, 155 : Better once than never, for never too late.

Publilius Syrus (1835), 612 : Non unquam sera est ad bonos mores via (It is never too late to take the road to rectitude). ❡*Ibid.*, 879:

Satius est sero te quam nunquam discere (It is better to learn late than never).

Cf. Tilley, *Eliz. Prov. Lore*, 377, *Prov. in Eng.*, L85.

170   TOO MUCH **LAUGHTER** IS TO BE AVOIDED

L. Lab. Lost, I, i, 199–200: To hear meekly, sir, and to laugh moderately, or to forbear both.

Culman, 3: Risum moderare (Moderate thy laughter). ¶*Ibid.*, 9: Risus nimius cavendus (Too much laughter is to be avoided).

171   **LEARN** FROM THE LEARNED

Cf. no. 39: Take counsel of the wise

As You Like It, III, ii, 69: Learn of the wise.

Culman, 26: Sapientia est a viro sapiente discere (It is wisdom to learn of a wise man).

Cato, *Disticha*, iv, 23: Disce sed a doctis (Learn from the learned).

¶Spenser, *Shep. Cal.*, Nov., 29: Learne of hem, that learned bee.

172   TOO MUCH **LENITY** ENCOURAGES
WRONGDOING

Cf. no. 145: To spare the guilty is to injure the innocent; no. 229:
Pardon makes offenders

3 Hen. VI, II, vi, 22: What makes robbers bold but too much lenity?
¶*Rom. & Jul.*, III, i, 202: Mercy but murders, pardoning those that kill. ¶*Meas. for Meas.*, I, iii, 37–39: For we bid this be done [bid people abuse their liberties], When evil deeds have their permissive pass And not the punishment.

* Publilius Syrus (1934), 277: Invitat culpam qui peccatum praeterit (He who passes over a sin invites wrongdoing). ¶*Ibid.*, 439: Nisi vindices delicta, improbitatem adiuves (If you didn't punish offenses, you'd help roguery). ¶*Ibid.*, 580: Qui ulcisci dubitat improbos plures facit (He makes rascals increase, who is reluctant to punish).

173   A **LIAR** SHOULD HAVE A GOOD MEMORY

Tempest, I, ii, 97–103: He ... Made such a sinner of his memory To credit his own lie, he did believe He was indeed the Duke.

Culman, 13: Mendacem memorem esse oportet (It behoves a liar to have a good memory).

Quintilian, *Inst. Orat.*, iv, 2, 91–92: Verumque est illud, quod vulgo dicitur, mendacem memorem esse oportere (And there is no doubt about the truth of the proverb that a liar should have a good memory). ¶Erasmus, *Adagia*, 514A: Mendacem memorem esse oportet (It is necessary for a liar to have a memory).

Cf. Tilley, *Prov. in Eng.*, L219.

174   TOO MUCH **LIBERTY** SPOILS ALL

Com. of Errors, II, i, 15: Headstrong liberty is lash'd with woe.

Culman, 14: Omnes deteriores sumus licentia (We are all worse by too much liberty).

Terence, *Heauton*, 483: Deteriores omnes sumus licentia (We all degenerate in the absence of control).

Cf. Bacon, *Promus*, 122; Tilley, *Prov. in Eng.*, L225.

175   A GOOD MAN HATES A **LIE**

Rich. II, I, i, 114: God and good men hate so foul a liar! ¶*Merry Wives*, I, i, 69–71: Shall I [Parson Evans] tell you a lie? I do despise a liar as I do despise one that is false, or as I despise one that is not true.

Culman, 22: Mendacium odit omnis sapiens & bonus (Every wise man and good man hateth a lie).

176   YOU OUGHT NOT TO **LIE**

Hen. VIII, IV, ii, 142–143: I dare avow (And now I should not lie), but will deserve.

Culman, 8: Nil mentiri debes (You ought not to lie).

Cato, *Collectio Dis. Vulg.*, 44: Nihil mentire (Tell no lie).

177   **LIFE** SEEMS LONG BECAUSE OF
                    ITS ILLS (SORROWS)

Lucrece, 990–991: Mark how slow time goes In time of sorrow. ¶ *Ibid.*,
1573: Short time seems long in sorrow's sharp sustaining. ¶ *Rom. &
Jul.*, I, i, 168: Sad hours seem long. ¶ *Rich. II*, I, iii, 261: Grief makes
one hour ten.

Publilius Syrus (1934), 92: Brevis ipsa vita est sed malis fit longior
(Life is short, but its ills make it seem long).

Lucian, *Greek Anthology*: *Epigr.*, x, 28: Τοῖσι μὲν εὖ πράττουσιν πᾶς
ὁ βίος βραχύς ἐστιν, τοῖς δὲ κακῶς μία νὺξ ἄπλετός ἐστι χρόνος (For
men who are fortunate all life is short, but for those who fall into
misfortune one night is infinite time).

178   AN ILL **LIFE**, AN ILL END

2 Hen. VI, II, iii, 104: For by his death we do perceive his guilt. ¶ *Ibid.*,
III, iii, 5–6: What a sign it is of evil life Where death's approach is seen
so terrible! ¶ *Ibid.*, 30: So bad a death argues a monstrous life.

Publilius Syrus (1835), 465: Male vivet quisquis nesciet mori bene
(He must have lived ill, who knows not how to die well).

Seneca, *De Tran.*, xi, 4: Male vivet quisquis nesciet bene mori (That
man will live ill who will not know how to die well).

Cf. Tilley, *Prov. in Eng.*, L247.

179   THE **LIFE** OF MAN IS SHORT

Cf. no. 191: Man is but a bubble

1 Hen. IV, V, ii, 82: The time of life is short!

Culman, 5: Brevis hominum vita (The life of man is short).

Seneca, *Epist.*, lxxvii, 20: Nulla vita est non brevis (There is no life that is not short). Erasmus, *Adagia*, 943B: Vita mortalium brevis (The life of man is short). Cf. *Colloquia Fam.*, 860D: Sed hominum vita brevis est (The life of man is short). (III, 173).

180 LIKE WILL TO LIKE

All's Well, I, i, 237–238: The mightiest space in fortune nature brings To join like likes and kiss like native things.

Culman, 24: Pares cum paribus facile congregantur (Like are easily gathered together with like). ¶ *Ibid.*, 27: Semper similem ducit Deus ad similem (God doth always bring like to like). ¶ Publilius Syrus (1835), 690: Plerumque similem ducit ad similem Deus (God generally finds a way for like to meet like).

Aristotle, *N. Ethics*, viii, 1, 6: ὅμοιον τοῦ ὁμοίου ἐφίεσθαι (Like seeks after like); cf. *Rhet.*, i, 11, 25. ¶ Cicero, *De Sen.*, iii, 7: Pares autem vetere proverbio cum paribus facillime congregantur (And according to the old adage, like with like most readily foregathers); cf. Quintilian, *Inst. Orat.*, v, 11, 41. ¶ Erasmus, *Adagia*, 79E: Simile gaudet simili (Like enjoys like); cf. 78D.

Cf. Udall, *Apoph. of Erasm.*, 215:22; Taverner, 8; Tilley, *Prov. in Eng.*, L286.

181 EVERYONE LIKES HIS OWN THINGS BEST

Rom. & Jul., I, ii, 104–105: I'll go along, no such sight to be shown, But to rejoice in splendour of mine own. ¶ *As You Like It*, V, iv, 60–61: A poor virgin, sir, an ill-favour'd thing, sir, but mine own. ¶ *Timon*, I, i, 170–171: Things of like value, differing in the owners, Are prized by their masters.

Culman, 9: Suum cuique pulchrum (Everyone likes his own things best).

Aristotle, *N. Ethics*, iv, 1, 20: πάντες ἀγαπῶσι μᾶλλον τὰ αὑτῶν ἔργα (Everybody is specially fond of a thing that is his own creation). ¶ Erasmus, *Adagia*, 74E: Suum cuique pulchrum (To each one, his own is beautiful).

Cf. Taverner, 7; Bacon, *Promus*, 981; Tilley, *Eliz. Prov. Lore*, 471, *Prov. in Eng.*, M131.

182 IT MATTERS NOT HOW LONG YOU **LIVE**
BUT HOW WELL

Coriol., III, i, 152–153: Prefer A noble life before a long.

Culman, 21: Laudatur, non qui diu, sed qui bene vixit (He is commended, not who hath lived long, but who hath lived well). ❡*Ibid.*, 22: Non refert quam diu vixeris, sed quam bene (It matters not how long you live, but how well). ❡Publilius Syrus (1835), 844: Refert, quam quis bene vivat; quam diu, non refert (It matters not how long you live but how well).

Seneca, *De Benef.*, iii, 31, 4: Non est bonum vivere, sed bene vivere (It is not a blessing to live, but to live well). ❡Seneca, *Epist.*, ci, 15: Quam bene vivas refert, non quam diu (The point is, not how long you live, but how nobly you live). ❡Erasmus, *Similia*, 586B: Laudatur . . . non qui diu vixit, sed qui bene (A man is not to be praised who lives long, but who lives well).

Cf. Tilley, *Eliz. Prov. Lore*, 398, *Prov. in Eng.*, L386.

183 THE **LONGER** THE LIFE,
THE GREATER THE MISERY

Rich. II, V, i, 90: So longest way shall have the longest moans.

Culman, 13: Longior vita, diuturna calamitas (A longer life is a long-lasting calamity). ❡*Ibid.*, 33: Longior vita, diuturna calamitas (The longer life is, a long-lasting misery). ❡Publilius Syrus (1835), 441: Longaeva vita mille fert molestias (A long life makes acquaintance with a thousand ills).

Cf. Tilley, *Prov. in Eng.*, L260.

184 THE **LOSS** THAT IS NOT KNOWN IS NO LOSS

Othello, III, iii, 342–343: He that is robb'd, not wanting what is stol'n, Let him not know't, and he's not robb'd at all.

* Publilius Syrus (1934), 161: Dimissum quod nescitur non amittitur (The loss that is not known is no loss).

Cf. Tilley, *Prov. in Eng.*, L461.

185   LOVE IS A SWEET TORMENT

Rom. & Jul., I, i, 186–189: Misshapen chaos of well-seeming forms!
Feather of lead, bright smoke, cold fire, sick health! . . . This love feel I.

Publilius Syrus (1934), 306: In venere semper certat dolor et gaudium
(In love, pain is ever at war with joy).

Plautus, *Cistellaria*, 69: Amor et melle et felle est fecundissimus
(Love is fairly overflowing with honey and gall both).

Cf. Tilley, *Prov. in Eng.*, L505a.

186   LOVE IS BRED BY LOOKING

Merch. of V., III, ii, 63–68: Tell me, where is fancy bred? . . . It is
engend'red in the eyes, With gazing fed. ¶ *Twelfth N.*, I, v, 315–317:
Methinks I feel this youth's perfections With an invisible and subtle
stealth To creep in at mine eyes.

Culman, 11: Amorem oculi potissimum conciliant (The eyes especially
win love). ¶ *Ibid.*, 12: Ex aspectu nascitur amor (Love is bred by looking
at one). ¶ Publilius Syrus (1934), 497: Oculi (occulte) amorem incipiunt,
consuetudo perficit (The eyes start love secretly: intimacy perfects it).

Ovid, *Artis Amat.*, iii, 510: Comibus est oculis alliciendus amor (By
gentle eyes must love be enticed). ¶ Erasmus, *Adagia*, 100E: Ex
adspectu nascitur amor (From looking love is born).

Cf. Taverner, 11; Tilley, *Eliz. Prov. Lore*, 408, *Prov. in Eng.*, L501.

**187   LOVE YOUR FRIEND,
BUT LOOK TO YOURSELF**

Timon, II, i, 23–24: I love and honour him, But must not break my
back to heal his finger.

Publilius Syrus (1934), 54: Amicis ita prodesto ne noceas tibi
(Benefit friends without hurt to yourself).

Cato, *Disticha*, i, 11: Dilige sic alios, ut sis tibi carus amicus; sic
bonus esto bonis, ne te mala damna sequantur (Love other men; yet be
your own true friend: Do good to good men so no loss attend).

188   COAXING, NOT COMPULSION,
                 MAKES **LOVE** SWEET

1 Hen. VI, V, v, 62: What is wedlock forced but a hell? ¶ *Two Gent.*, V,
ii, 7: Love will not be spurr'd to what it loathes.

   * Publilius Syrus (1934), 69: Blanditia non imperio fit dulcis venus
(Coaxing, not ordering, makes love sweet).

   Cf. Tilley, *Prov. in Eng.*, L499.

189   IN THE SAME HEART **LOVE** AND
                 FEAR CANNOT THRIVE

Lucrece, 270: Love thrives not in the heart that shadows dreadeth.

   Publilius Syrus (1835), 40: Amor misceri cum timore non potest
(Love and fear cannot mix).

   Seneca, *Epist.*, xlvii, 18: Non potest amor cum timore misceri (Love
and fear cannot be mingled).

190   IT IS IMPOSSIBLE TO **LOVE** AND BE WISE

Troilus & Cres., III, ii, 162–164: But you are wise, Or else you love not;
for to be wise and love Exceeds man's might: that dwells with gods
above.

   * Publilius Syrus (1934), 22: Amare et sapere vix deo conceditur
(Wisdom with love is scarcely granted to a god). ¶ *Ibid.*, 131: Cum
ames non sapias aut cum sapias non ames (Love means you can't be
wise: wisdom means you can't be in love).

   Erasmus, *Adagia*, 476E: Amare et sapere, vix Deo conceditur (To
love and to be wise is scarcely granted to God).

   Cf. Malone, *Variorum* (1821), VIII, 332; Tilley, *Eliz. Prov. Lore*, 692,
Prov. in Eng., L558; Baldwin, I, 604.

191   **MAN** IS BUT A BUBBLE

      Cf. no. 179: The life of man is short

Rich. III, IV, iv, 82–90: I call'd thee then . . . A dream of what thou
wast . . . a breath, a bubble.

Culman, 28: Vita nostra similis bullae in aqua (Our life is like a bubble on the water).

Varro, *De Re Rustica*, i, 1, 1: Ut dicitur, si est homo bulla (If man is a bubble, as the proverb has it). ¶ Erasmus, *Adagia*, 500A: Homo bulla (Man is a bubble).

Cf. Taverner, 33; Stevenson, 1509:6; Tilley, *Prov. in Eng.*, M246.

192   MAN IS BY NATURE WICKED

Timon, IV, iii, 19–20: There's nothing level in our cursed natures But direct villany.

Culman, 33: Hominis cor ex natura sua malum (Man's heart is wicked of its own nature).

193   MARRY WITH YOUR MATCH

Twelfth N., I, iii, 115–117: She'll none o' th' Count. She'll not match above her degree, neither in estate, years, nor wit.

Culman, 11: Conjugium inaequalium malum est (The matching of unequal parties is bad).

Ovid, *Heroides*, ix, 32: Siqua voles apte nubere, nube pari (Would you be wedded happily, wed your equal). ¶ Erasmus, *Adagia*, 301D: Aequalem uxorem quaere (Seek a wife who is your equal).

Cf. Taverner, 61; Bacon, *Promus*, 1111; Tilley, *Prov. in Eng.*, E178.

194   THE REQUEST OF A MASTER
IS A COMMAND

Com. of Errors, IV, i, 112–113: Thither I must, although against my will, For servants must their masters' minds fulfil. ¶ *K. Lear*, V, iii, 322: My master calls me; I must not say no.

Publilius Syrus (1835), 146: Cogit rogando, quum rogat potentior (The request of a master is a command).

195   IN ALL THINGS THE **MEAN** IS THE BEST

Cf. no. 196: There is measure in all things; no. 208: Be moderate in
all things

Merch. of V., I, ii, 7–8: It is no mean happiness, therefore, to be seated
in the mean. ¶ *Much Ado*, II, i, 7–9: He were an excellent man that were
made just in the midway between him and Benedick.

Culman, 21: Modus omnibus in rebus optimus habendus (A mean is
to be accounted the best in all things).

Aristotle, *N. Ethics*, ii, 9, 1: ἡ ἀρετὴ ἡ ἠθικὴ μεσότης (Moral virtue
is a mean).

Cf. Udall, *Apoph. of Erasm.*, 55:20; 98:42; Bacon, *Promus*, 87.

196   THERE IS **MEASURE** IN ALL THINGS

Cf. no. 195: In all things the mean is the best; no. 208: Be moderate
in all things

Much Ado, II, i, 74–75: There is measure in everything.

Culman, 10: Adest unicuique rei modus (Everything hath a measure).

Horace, *Sat.*, i, 1, 106: Est modus in rebus (There is measure in all
things).

Cf. Tilley, *Prov. in Eng.*, M806.

197   A MAN'S **MIND** OFTEN GIVES HIM WARNING

Rom. & Jul., I, iv, 106–107: My mind misgives Some consequence,
yet hanging in the stars. ¶ *Rich. III*, II, iii, 42–43: By a divine instinct
men's minds mistrust Ensuing danger. ¶ *Ibid.*, V, iii, 73–74: I have not
that alacrity of spirit Nor cheer of mind that I was wont to have.
¶ *Much Ado*, III, iv, 24–25: God give me joy to wear it [wedding gown]!
for my heart is exceeding heavy. ¶ *Hamlet*, V, ii, 222–224: But thou
wouldst not think how ill all's here about my heart. But it is no matter.
¶ *Ant. & Cleop.*, IV, xiv, 120–121: She had a prophesying fear Of what
hath come to pass. ¶ *Cymb.*, IV, ii, 110–111: He had not apprehension
Of roaring terrors.

Culman, 7: Mens praesaga futuri (The mind is foreknowing of a thing to come). ¶ *Ibid.*, 13: Mens est praesaga futuri (The mind is a foreteller of that which is to come).
Cf. Tilley, *Prov. in Eng.*, M475.

198   THE MIND ALWAYS FEARS THE UNKNOWN EVIL MORE

Hamlet, III, i, 78–82: The dread of something after death . . . makes us rather bear those ills we have Than fly to others that we know not of.
Publilius Syrus (1934), 655: Semper plus metuit animus ignotum malum (The mind always fears the unknown evil more).
Cf. Tilley, *Prov. in Eng.*, H166.

199   THE MARRIAGE OF TRUE MINDS IS THE STRONGEST OF TIES

Troilus & Cres., II, iii, 110–111: The amity that wisdom knits not, folly may easily untie. ¶ *Sonnets*, 116, 1–2: Let me not to the marriage of true minds Admit impediments.
Publilius Syrus (1934), 529: Perenne coniugium animus, non corpus, facit (Mind, not body, makes lasting wedlock). ¶ * *Ibid.* (1835), 149: Conjunctio animi maxima est cognatio (The marriage of true minds is the strongest of ties).
Erasmus, *Colloquia Fam.*, 696A: Magis erit animorum quam corporum conjugium (The wedlock of minds will be greater than that of bodies).

200   MEN ARE PRONE TO MISCHIEF

Rom. & Jul., V, i, 35–36: O mischief, thou art swift To enter in the thoughts of desperate men! ¶ *Hen. VIII*, I, i, 160–161: He is subtile, and as prone to mischief As able to perform't.
Culman, 12: Homines ad malum proclives (Men are prone to mischief).

201 THE **MISER** LACKS WHAT HE HAS AS MUCH
AS WHAT HE HASN'T

Lucrece, 134–140: Those that much covet are with gain so fond For what they have not, that which they possess, They scatter and unloose it from their bond, And so, by hoping more, they have but less; Or, gaining more, the profit of excess Is but to surfeit, and such griefs sustain That they prove bankrout in this poor rich gain.

* Publilius Syrus (1934), 694: Tam deest avaro quod habet quam quod non habet (The miser lacks what he has as much as what he hasn't).

Quintilian, *Inst. Orat.*, viii, 5, 6: Tam deest avaro, quod habet, quam quod non habet (The miser lacks that which he has no less than what he has not); cf. ix, 3, 64.

Cf. Malone, *Variorum* (1821), XX, 110; Baldwin, I, 604.

202 **MISERY** NEVER QUITS HIM WHOSE
THOUGHTS ALWAYS RUN WITH HIS FEARS

Tempest, II, i, 16–19: When every grief is entertain'd that's offer'd, Comes to th' entertainer . . . Dolour comes to him, indeed.

Publilius Syrus (1934), 458: Numquam non miser est qui quod timeat cogitat (Misery never quits him whose thoughts run on something to dread).

203 PAST HAPPINESS AUGMENTS PRESENT **MISERY**

Rich. III, IV, iv, 116–119: O thou well skill'd in curses, stay awhile And teach me how to curse mine enemies! . . . Compare dead happiness with living woe.

Publilius Syrus (1835), 100: Bis ille miser est, ante qui felix fuit (Past happiness augments present wretchedness).

Cf. Tilley, *Eliz. Prov. Lore*, 318, *Prov. in Eng.*, M1010.

204 **MISFORTUNE** SELDOM COMES ALONE

Rich. II, III, iv, 28: Woe is forerun with woe. ¶ *Hamlet*, IV, v, 78-79: When sorrows come, they come not single spies, But in battalions!

❡*Ibid.*, vii, 165: One woe doth tread upon another's heel. ❡*Pericles*, I, iv, 63–64: One sorrow never comes but brings an heir That may succeed as his inheritor.

Culman, 15: Raro ulla calamitas est sola (There is seldom any calamity alone).

Erasmus, *Adagia*, 1208E: Mala malis eveniunt (With evils evils come).

Cf. Tilley, *Prov. in Eng.*, M1012.

205   EVERYONE MAKES **MISTAKES**

Cf. no. 98: Everyone has his faults; no. 333: No one is wise at all times

Rich. III, IV, iv, 292–293: Men shall deal unadvisedly sometimes, Which after-hours gives leisure to repent.

Culman, 12: Errare commune est mortalibus (It is a common thing for men to make mistakes).

206   THE EYES AND EARS OF THE **MOB** ARE OFTEN FALSE WITNESSES

Hamlet, IV, iii, 4–7: The distracted multitude . . . like not in their judgment, but their eyes; And where 'tis so, th' offender's scourge is weigh'd, But never the offence.

Culman, 10: Vulgi judicium stultum (The judgment of the common people is fond). ❡Publilius Syrus (1835), 867: Saepe oculi et aures vulgi sunt testes mali (The eyes and ears of the mob are often false witnesses).

207   **MOCK** NO ONE

Much Ado, I, i, 287: Nay, mock not, mock not. ❡*Hamlet*, II, ii, 571: Look you mock him not. ❡*K. Lear*, IV, vii, 59: Pray, do not mock me. ❡*Ant. & Cleop.*, IV, vi, 25: Mock not, Enobarbus.

Culman, 2: Neminem irriseris (Mock nobody).

Cato, *Collectio Dis. Vulg.*, 31: Neminem riseris (Mock no one).

Cf. Tilley, *Prov. in Eng.*, M1313.

208 BE **MODERATE** IN ALL THINGS

Cf. no. 195 : In all things the mean is the best; no. 196: There is measure in all things

Merch. of V., III, ii, 111–112: Be moderate; allay thy ecstasy; In measure rain thy joy; scant this excess! ¶ *Hamlet*, III, ii, 6–9: In the very torrent, tempest, and (as I may say) whirlwind of your passion, you must acquire and beget a temperance that may give it smoothness. ¶ *Troilus & Cres.*, IV, iv, 1 : Be moderate, be moderate. ¶ *Ant. & Cleop.*, V, ii, 48–49: O, temperance, lady! —Sir, I will eat no meat; I'll not drink. ¶ *Tempest*, IV, i, 53: Be more abstemious. ¶ *Hen. VIII*, I, i, 123–125: What, are you chaf'd? Ask God for temp'rance. That's th' appliance only Which your disease requires.

Culman, 3 : Temperantiam exerce (Use temperance). ¶ *Ibid.*, 8: Ne quid nimis (Do nothing too much). ¶ *Ibid.*, 23 : Omne nimium cunctis in rebus est fugiendum (Everything that is too much is to be avoided in all things).

Plato, *Gorgias*, 507D: τὸν βουλόμενον, ὡς ἔοικεν, εὐδαίμονα εἶναι σωφροσύνην μὲν διωκτέον καὶ ἀσκητέον (Anyone, as it seems, who desires to be happy must pursue and practice temperance). ¶ Aristotle, *Rhet.*, ii, 21, 13 : Μηδὲν ἄγαν (Nothing in excess). ¶ Plautus, *Poenulus*, 237: Modus omnibus rebus (Moderation in all things). ¶ Terence, *Andria*, 61 : Ne quid nimis (Moderation in all things). ¶ Cicero, *De Fin.*, iii, 22, 73 : Nihil nimis (Moderation in all things). ¶ Seneca, *Epist.*, xciv, 43: Nil nimis (Nothing in excess). ¶ Erasmus, *Adagia*, 259E: Ne quid nimis (Nothing too much).

Cf. Taverner, 19; Stevenson, 1602:1–4.

209 **MONEY** MASTERS ALL THINGS

Cf. no. 142: When gold argues the cause, eloquence is impotent

Cymb., II, iii, 72–78: 'Tis gold Which buys admittance . . . What Can it not do and undo?

Culman, 5 : Auro nihil inexpugnabile (Nothing is unconquerable with gold). ¶ *Ibid.*, 27: Sola pecunia possunt expugnari alioqui invicta (Things otherwise invincible may be overcome only with money).

Euripides, *Phoenissae*, 439–440: τὰ χρήματ' ἀνθρώποισι τιμιώτατα δύναμίν τε πλείστην τῶν ἐν ἀνθρώποις ἔχει (Wealth in men's eyes is honored most of all, and of all things on earth has chiefest power). ¶Erasmus, *Adagia*, 144D: Pecuniae obediunt omnia (All things obey money).

Cf. Udall, *Apoph. of Erasm.*, 188:13; Taverner, 14; Stevenson, 1618:2; Tilley, *Prov. in Eng.*, M1102.

210   THE MORE A MAN HAS, THE MORE
HE DESIRES

Lucrece, 97–98: But, poorly rich, so wanteth in his store That, cloy'd with much, he pineth still for more. ¶*Ibid.*, 151–152: In having much, torments us with defect Of that we have. ¶*L. Lab. Lost*, IV, iii, 237: Where nothing wants that want itself doth seek. ¶*Macb.*, IV, iii, 81–82: My more-having would be as a sauce To make me hunger more.

Publilius Syrus (1934), 55: Avarus animus nullo satiatur lucro (No gain satisfies a greedy mind). ¶*Ibid.* (1835), 71: Avarum irritat, non satiat pecunia (Money does not sate avarice, but stimulates it).

Lucretius, *De Rerum Natura*, iv, 1089–1090: Plurima habemus, tum magis ardescit dira cuppedine pectus (The more we have the more fierce burns the heart with fell craving). ¶Horace, *Odes*, iii, 16, 42–43: Multa petentibus desunt multa (To those who seek for much, much is ever lacking). ¶Horace, *Epist.*, ii, 2, 147–148: Quanto plura parasti, tanto plura cupis (The more you get, the more you want). ¶Ovid, *Fasti*, i, 212: Cum possideant plurima, plura petunt (They who have the most possessions still crave for more). ¶Seneca, *De Benef.*, ii, 27, 3: Maiora cupimus, quo maiora venerunt (The more we get, the more we covet). ¶Seneca, *Epist.*, cxix, 6: Qui multum habet, plus cupit (He who has much desires more).

Cf. Tilley, *Prov. in Eng.*, M1144, M1287.

211   NATURE HAS GIVEN A DEFECT TO
EVERYTHING CREATED

Hamlet, I, iv, 30–32: These men Carrying, I say, the stamp of one defect, Being nature's livery, or fortune's star.

Culman, 28: Unicuique dedit vitium natura creato (Nature hath given a defect to everything created).

212 NATURE PASSES NURTURE

Tempest, IV, i, 188–189: A devil, a born devil, on whose nature Nurture can never stick!

Culman, 25: Quod natura est insitum, nullo corriges negotio (You can correct by no pains, that which is inbred by nature).

Cf. Tilley, *Prov. in Eng.*, N47.

213 NATURE WILL HAVE HER COURSE

Titus Andr. (Q. 2 and Ff.), V, iii, 168: Kind nature doth require it so. ¶*Hamlet*, IV, vii, 189: Nature her custom holds. ¶*Cymb.*, III, iii, 79: How hard it is to hide the sparks of nature!

Culman, 5: Difficillimum vincere naturam (It is a very hard thing to conquer nature). ¶*Ibid.*, 8: Natura frustra repugnatur (It is in vain to resist nature). ¶*Ibid.*, 23: Naturae suum jus eripere difficile est (It is an hard thing to take from nature its own right).

Cf. Tilley, *Prov. in Eng.*, N48.

214 THE NATURE OF A MAN IS REVEALED BY HIS SPEECH

Tempest, I, ii, 496–497: My father's of a better nature, sir, Than he appears by speech.

Culman, 12: Hominis figura oratione cognoscitur (The fashion of a man is known by his speech). ¶*Ibid.*, 16: Sermone qualitas viri cognoscitur (A man's quality is known by his talk). ¶*Ibid.*: Ut quisque est, ita loquitur (As everyone is, so he speaketh). ¶Publilius Syrus (1835), 1092: Sermo imago animi est: vir qualis, talis est oratio (Speech is a mirror of the soul; as a man speaks, so is he).

Menander, *The Flute Girl*, 72K: ἀνδρὸς χαρακτὴρ ἐκ λόγου γνωρίζεται (A man's character is revealed by his speech); cf. *The Self-Tormentor*,

143K. ¶ Cato, *Disticha*, iv, 20: Sermo hominum mores et celat et indicat idem (The talk of men at the same time conceals and reveals their character). ¶ Cicero, *Tusc. Disp.*, v, 16, 47: Qualis autem homo ipse esset, talem eius esse orationem (As was the man in himself so was his speech). ¶ Seneca, *Epist.*, cxiv, 2: Talis hominibus fuit oratio qualis vita (Man's speech is just like his life).

Cf. Udall, *Apoph. of Erasm.*, 31:71; 90:28; Taverner, 18; Stevenson, 2183:2; Tilley, *Prov. in Eng.*, M75.

215   TO SUBMIT TO **NECESSITY** INVOLVES NO DISGRACE

K. Lear, I, iv, 231–233: Offence Which else were shame, that . . . necessity Must call discreet proceeding.

Culman, 17: Abjiciendus pudor quoties urget necessitas (Shame is to be thrown away, as often as necessity constrains). ¶ * Publilius Syrus (1934), 256: Honeste servit qui succumbit tempori (To yield to the need of the time is honorable service).

Plautus, *Asinaria*, 671: Quidvis egestas imperat (Need knows no shame).

216   **NEGLECT** A DANGER, AND IT WILL TAKE YOU BY SURPRISE

Cf. no. 322: Good watch prevents misfortune

1 Hen. VI, IV, iii, 49: Sleeping neglection doth betray to loss.

* Publilius Syrus (1934), 107: Citius venit periclum cum contemnitur (Danger comes more quickly when underestimated). ¶ *Ibid.*, 617: Quod est timendum decipit si neglegas (The object of your fear tricks you, if you overlook it).

217   HE HAS ILL **NEIGHBORS** THAT IS FAIN TO PRAISE HIMSELF

Titus Andr., V, iii, 116–118: But soft! methinks I do digress too much, Citing my worthless praise. O, pardon me! For when no friends are by, men praise themselves. ¶ *Much Ado*, V, ii, 76–79: There's not one wise man among twenty that will praise himself. —An old, an old instance, Beatrice, that liv'd in the time of good neighbours. ¶ *Hamlet*, V, ii, 189–192: I commend my duty to your lordship. —Yours, yours. [*Exit Osric.*] He does well to commend it himself; there are no tongues else for's turn.

Culman, 26: Qui de se praedicant arrogantius, malos habent vicinos (They that vaunt proudly of themselves, have bad neighbours).

Cf. Tilley, *Prov. in Eng.*, N117.

218   **NIGHT** IS THE NURSE OF BASE THINGS

Venus & A., 773: Black-fac'd night, desire's foul nurse. ¶ *Jul. Caesar*, II, i, 78–79: By night . . . evils are most free.

Culman, 23: Nox, amor, vinum, turpia suadent (The night, love, and wine do persuade filthy things).

Cf. Tilley, *Prov. in Eng.*, O70.

219 **NOTHING** IS WELL SAID OR DONE IN ANGER

Cf. no. 9: He invites danger who indulges in anger

2 Hen. VI, I, iii, 155–157: Now, lords, my choler being overblown With walking once about the quadrangle, I come to talk of commonwealth affairs. ¶ *1 Hen. IV*, I, i, 105–107: But come yourself with speed to us again; For more is to be said and to be done Than out of anger can be uttered. ¶ *2 Hen. IV*, I, i, 161–162: This strained passion doth you wrong, my lord. —Sweet Earl, divorce not wisdom from your honour.

Culman, 5: Consilio inimica iracundia (Anger is an enemy to counsel). ¶ *Ibid.*, 13: Irati nihil recte faciunt (Angry folks do nothing well). ¶ *Ibid.*, 24: Pessimi sunt consultores ira & cupido (Anger and lust are the worst advisers). ¶ Publilius Syrus (1835), 178: Cupido atque ira consultores pessimi (Anger and inordinate desire are the worst of counselors).

Cicero, *De Offic.*, i, 38, 136: Cum qua nihil recte fieri, nihil considerate potest (For in anger nothing right or judicious can be done).
Cf. Tilley, *Prov. in Eng.*, N307.

220   A LOVER'S **OATH** INVOLVES NO PENALTY

Rom. & Jul., II, ii, 92–93: At lovers' perjuries, They say Jove laughs. ❡*L. Lab. Lost*, IV, iii, 63: Vows for thee broke deserve not punishment.

Publilius Syrus (1934), 37: Amantis ius iurandum poenam non habet (A lover's oath involves no penalty).

Hesiod, *Aegimius*, 3: ἐπισπᾶσθαι τὴν ἀπὸ τῶν θεῶν ὀργὴν τοὺς γινομένους ὅρκους ὑπὲρ ἔρωτος (Oaths touching the matter of love do not draw down anger from the gods). ❡Ovid, *Artis Amat.*, i, 633: Iuppiter ex alto periuria ridet amantum (Jupiter from on high laughs at the perjuries of lovers). ❡Erasmus, *Adagia*, 549C: Venereum jusjurandum non punitur (The oath of a lover is not punished).
Cf. Tilley, *Eliz. Prov. Lore*, 360, *Prov. in Eng.*, J82.

221   KEEP THY **OATH**

3 Hen. VI, III, i, 90: Do not break your oaths. ❡*L. Lab. Lost*, I, i, 114: I'll keep what I have swore. ❡*T. of Shrew*, IV, ii, 36: That I may surely keep mine oath. ❡*Rich. II*, I, iii, 182: Keep the oath that we administer. ❡*Merch. of V.*, II, ix, 77: I'll keep my oath. ❡*Hen. V*, V, ii, 402: And may our oaths well kept and prosp'rous be! ❡*Jul. Caesar*, V, iii, 40: Keep thine oath. ❡*Twelfth N.*, III, iv, 341: Pray God he keep his oath!

Culman, 2: Jusjurandum serva (Keep thy oath).

Cato, *Collectio Dis. Vulg.*, 21: Iusiurandum serva (Keep an oath).

222   THROUGH **OBEDIENCE** A WOMAN
RULES HER HUSBAND

Cymb., III, iv, 157–158: You must forget to be a woman; change Command into obedience. ❡*Hen. VIII*, II, iv, 138–139: Wifelike government, Obeying in commanding.

*Publilius Syrus (1934), 108: Casta ad virum matrona parendo imperat (The chaste matron of her husband's home rules through obedience).

Sidney, *Arcadia*, *Works* (Feuillerat), I, 420: He ruling, because she would obey; or rather because she would obey, she therein ruling.

223 OBEY YOUR PARENTS

K. Lear, III, iv, 82–83: Obey thy parents.

Culman, 35: Parentibus obedire debemus (We ought to obey our parents).

224 OBLIVION IS OUR ONLY REMEDY FOR LOSSES

Hamlet, III, ii, 202–203: Most necessary 'tis that we forget To pay ourselves what to ourselves is debt.

Publilius Syrus (1835), 853: Rerum amissarum remedium est oblivio (Forgetfulness is our only relief against losses).

225 IT IS OFTEN BETTER TO OVERLOOK AN INJURY THAN TO AVENGE IT

Cf. no. 345: To forget a wrong is the best remedy

Timon, III, v, 39: To revenge is no valour, but to bear.

Publilius Syrus (1835), 1088: Saepe dissimulare, quam vel ulcisci, satius est (It is often better to overlook an injury than to avenge it).

Seneca, *De Ira*, ii, 33, 1: Saepe autem satius fuit dissimulare quam ulcisci (It is often, however, better to feign ignorance of an act than to take vengeance for it).

226 PAIN FORCES EVEN THE INNOCENT TO LIE

Cymb., III, vi, 9–13: Will poor folks lie, That have afflictions on them, knowing 'tis A punishment or trial? Yes . . . lie for need.

* Publilius Syrus (1934), 174: Etiam innocentes cogit mentiri dolor (Pain forces even the innocent to lie).

227 PAIN (GRIEF, LOVE) THAT HAS NO VOICE AMID TORTURE IS A HELL

Cf. no. 144: Mute grief feels a keener pang than that which cries aloud; no. 277: Speech is a cure for sorrow

Venus & A., 329–330: The heart hath treble wrong When it is barr'd the aidance of the tongue. ¶*Lucrece*, 1287–1288: Deep torture may be call'd a hell When more is felt than one hath power to tell. ¶*Ibid.*, 1462–1463: He did her wrong To give her so much grief and not a tongue. ¶*Hamlet*, I, ii, 159: But break my heart, for I must hold my tongue! ¶*Twelfth N.*, II, iv, 113–115: She never told her love, But let concealment, like a worm i' th' bud, Feed on her damask cheek. ¶*Macb.*, IV, iii, 209–210: Give sorrow words. The grief that does not speak Whispers the o'erfraught heart and bids it break.

* Publilius Syrus (1934), 248: Heu dolor quam miser est qui in tormento vocem non habet (How pitiful the pain that has no voice amid torture)!

Ovid, *Tristia*, v, 1, 63: Strangulat inclusus dolor atque exaestuat intus (A suppressed sorrow chokes and seethes within).

Cf. Tilley, *Prov. in Eng.*, G449.

228 NO PAINS, NO GAINS

Macb., IV, i, 39–40: O, well done! I commend your pains, And every one shall share i' th' gains.

Culman, 15: Parsimonia & labore crescunt res (Goods increase by sparing and pains).

Cf. Tilley, *Prov. in Eng.*, P24.

229 PARDON MAKES OFFENDERS

Cf. no. 145: To spare the guilty is to injure the innocent; no. 172: Too much lenity encourages wrongdoing

Lucrece, 1687: Sparing justice feeds iniquity. ¶ *Meas. for Meas.*, II, i, 298: Pardon is still the nurse of second woe. ¶ *Timon*, III, v, 3: Nothing emboldens sin so much as mercy.

Publilius Syrus (1934), 587: Qui culpae ignoscit uni suadet pluribus (To pardon one offense is to prompt more offenders). ¶ *Ibid.* (1835), 865: Saepe ignoscendo das injuriae locum (Repeated pardons encourage offenses).
Cf. Tilley, *Prov. in Eng.*, P50.

230   **PASSION** BLINDS THE EYE OF REASON

Othello, II, iii, 206-207: Passion, having my best judgment collied, Assays to lead the way.
Culman, 32: Furor depravat judicia (Rage depraveth the judgment). ¶ Publilius Syrus (1835), 1063: Nil rationis est, ubi res semel in affectum venit (Reason avails nothing when passion has the mastery).
Euripides, *Medea*, 1079: θυμὸς δὲ κρείσσων τῶν ἐμῶν βουλευμάτων (Passion overmasters sober thought). ¶ Cato, *Disticha*, ii, 4: Impedit ira animum, ne possis cernere verum (Temper bars minds from seeing what is true). ¶ Cicero, *Tusc. Disp.*, iii, 5, 11: Furorem autem esse rati sunt mentis ad omnia caecitatem (Frenzy, however, they regarded as a blindness of the mind in all relations). ¶ Quintilian, *Inst. Orat.*, vi, 2, 6: Sensum oculorum praecipit animus (Passion forestalls the sense of sight).

231   **PATIENCE** OF MIND HAS SECRET WEALTH

Othello, II, iii, 376: How poor are they that have not patience!
Publilius Syrus (1934), 504: Patientia animi occultas divitias habet (Patience of mind has secret wealth).

232   FAT **PAUNCHES** MAKE LEAN PATES

L. Lab. Lost, I, i, 26: Fat paunches have lean pates.
Culman, 24: Pinguis venter non gignit sensum tenuem (A fat belly doth not beget a fine wit).

Erasmus, *Adagia*, 853C: Pinguis venter non gignit sensum tenuem (A fat belly does not engender a sharp wit).
Cf. Baldwin, I, 592; Tilley, *Prov. in Eng.*, P123.

233   BITTER **PILLS** MAY HAVE WHOLESOME EFFECTS

Cf. no. 5: Afflictions are sent us by God for our good

Meas. for Meas., IV, vi, 7–8: 'Tis a physic That's bitter to sweet end.
Culman, 35: Piis condiuntur dulcia amaris (Sweet things are seasoned with bitter for the godly).
Cf. Tilley, *Prov. in Eng.*, P327.

234   **POVERTY** ROBS US OF OUR FRIENDS

Cf. no. 244: Prosperity makes friends, adversity tries them

As You Like It, II, i, 51–52: Misery doth part The flux of company.
¶ *Hen. VIII*, II, i, 127–130: For those you make friends And give your hearts to, when they once perceive The least rub in your fortunes, fall away Like water from ye.
Culman, 8: Paupertas amicis nos spoliat (Poverty bereaves us of friends).
Erasmus, *Adagia*, 1000E: Mendico ne parentes quidem amici sunt (In poverty not even parents are friends).
Cf. Tilley, *Prov. in Eng.*, P529.

235   **PRACTICE** MAKES MASTERY

Two Gent., I, iii, 22–23: Experience is by industry achiev'd And perfected by the swift course of time. ¶ *Hamlet*, V, ii, 221–222: I have been in continual practice. I shall win at the odds.
Culman, 5: Exercitatio potest omnia (Exercise can do all things).
¶ *Ibid.*, 10: Assidua exercitatio omnia potest (Daily exercise can do all things).

Erasmus, *Adagia*, 466A: Exercitatio potest omnia (Exercise can do all things).

Cf. Taverner, 30; Bacon, *Promus*, 958; Smith, 684; Tilley, *Prov. in Eng.*, U24.

236   **PRACTICE** WHAT YOU PREACH

Merch. of V., I, ii, 15–16: It is a good divine that follows his own instructions. ¶ *Hamlet*, I, iii, 47–51: Do not as some ungracious pastors do, Show me the steep and thorny way to heaven, Whiles, like a puff'd and reckless libertine, Himself the primrose path of dalliance treads And recks not his own rede.

Publilius Syrus (1835), 647: Orationi vita ne dissentiat (There should be no disagreement between our lives and our doctrines).

Plautus, *Persa*, 287: Quod dicis facere non quis (You preach what you can't practice)! ¶ Plautus, *Asinaria*, 644: Proinde istud facias ipse quod faciamus nobis suades (So you go on and practice yourself what you preach to us). ¶ Seneca, *De Vita Beata*, xx, 1: Non praestant philosophi quae loquuntur (Philosophers do not practice what they preach).

Cf. Tilley, *Prov. in Eng.*, P537a.

237   **PRAISE** IS THE REWARD OF VIRTUE

Cf. no. 239: Good things should be praised

Winter's T., I, ii, 91–94: Cram's with praise . . . One good deed dying tongueless Slaughters a thousand waiting upon that. Our praises are our wages.

Culman, 7: Laus merces virtutis (Praise is the reward of virtue).

238   DO NOT **PRAISE** YOUR OWN THINGS

Merch. of V., III, iv, 22–23: This comes too near the praising of myself. Therefore no more of it.

Culman, 8: Ne tua jactato (Do not brag of thine own things).
Cf. Tilley, *Prov. in Eng.*, M476.

239   GOOD THINGS SHOULD BE PRAISED

Cf. no. 237: Praise is the reward of virtue

Two Gent., III, i, 353–354: Good things should be praised.
Culman, 2: Laudato honesta (Praise honest things).

**240   THE GREATER THE PRICE, THE GREATER
THE PLEASURE**

Tempest, I, ii, 450–452: This swift business I must uneasy make, lest too
light winning Make the prize light.

Publilius Syrus (1934), 573: Quod vix contingit ut voluptatem parit
(What pleasure is produced by what is won with difficulty)! ¶ *Ibid.*, 700:
Voluptas e difficili data dulcissima est (Out of difficulty comes the
sweetest pleasure).

Aristotle, *Rhet.*, i, 7, 15: τὸ χαλεπώτερον τοῦ ῥᾴονος (That which is
more difficult is preferable to that which is easier of attainment).
¶ Juvenal, *Sat.*, xi, 16: Magis illa iuvant quae pluris emuntur (The
greater the price, the greater the pleasure).

Cf. Tilley, *Prov. in Eng.*, T201.

241   PRIDE IS THE VICE OF PROSPERITY

Coriol., IV, vii, 37–39: Pride . . . out of daily fortune ever taints The
happy man.

Culman, 5: Divitiae fastum pariunt (Riches bring forth haughtiness).
¶ Publilius Syrus (1835), 1004: Vitium sollemne fortunae est superbia
(Pride is prosperity's common vice).

242   LIKE PRINCE, LIKE PEOPLE

Lucrece, 615–616: For princes are the glass, the school, the book, Where
subjects' eyes do learn, do read, do look. ¶ *Hamlet*, III, i, 158–161: O,
what a noble mind is here o'erthrown! . . . The glass of fashion and
the mould of form.

Culman, 15: Qualis princeps, talis populus (Such a prince, such a people).
Cf. Tilley, *Prov. in Eng.*, K70.

243   GREAT **PROMISE**, SMALL PERFORMANCE

Rom. & Jul., II, iv, 155–157: A gentleman, nurse, that loves to hear himself talk and will speak more in a minute than he will stand to in a month. ¶ *Troilus & Cres.*, III, ii, 91–95: All lovers swear more performance than they are able . . . vowing more than the perfection of ten, and discharging less than the tenth part of one. ¶ *Othello*, IV, ii, 184–185: Your words and performance are no kin together. ¶ *Hen. VIII*, IV, ii, 41–42: His promises were, as he then was, mighty; But his performance, as he is now, nothing.

Publilius Syrus (1835), 537: Ne plus promittas, quam praestari possiet (Never promise more than you can perform).

Cato, *Disticha*, i, 25: Quod dare non possis, verbis promittere noli (Never promise what you cannot perform).

Cf. Tilley, *Prov. in Eng.*, P602.

244   **PROSPERITY** MAKES FRIENDS, ADVERSITY
TRIES THEM

Cf. no. 234: Poverty robs us of our friends

Winter's T., IV, iv, 584: Prosperity's the very bond of love.

Publilius Syrus (1835), 887: Secundae amicos res parant, tristes probant (Prosperity makes friends, adversity tries them). ¶ * *Ibid.*, 1044: Ipsae amicos res opimae pariunt, adversae probant (Prosperity makes friends; adversity tests them).

Cf. Tilley, *Prov. in Eng.*, P611.

245   MAN'S **PRUDENCE** IS A PART
OF HIS FORTUNE

Ant. & Cleop., III, xiii, 31–32: Men's judgments are A parcel of their fortunes.

*Publilius Syrus (1835), 276: Fortuna nulli plus quam consilium valet (Fortune has no more power over our destiny than our own actions).

246   IT IS **RARITY** THAT GIVES ZEST TO PLEASURE

1 Hen. IV, III, ii, 57–59: And so my state, Seldom but sumptuous, show'd like a feast And won by rareness such solemnity. ¶*Sonnets*, 52, 2–7: His sweet up-locked treasure . . . he will not ev'ry hour survey, For blunting the fine point of seldom pleasure. Therefore are feasts so solemn and so rare, Since, seldom coming, in the long year set, Like stones of worth they thinly placed are.

Culman, 16: Voluptates commendat rarior usus (The more seldom use commendeth pleasures). ¶Publilius Syrus (1934), 630: Rarum esse oportet quod diu carum velis (Rare must be that which you would long hold dear).

Juvenal, *Sat.*, xi, 208: Voluptates commendat rarior usus (It is rarity that gives zest to pleasure). ¶Erasmus, *Colloquia Fam.*, 888B: Voluptates commendat rarior usus (Rare use commends pleasures).

247   LET **REASON** RULE YOUR ACTIONS

Mids. Night's D., II, ii, 115–116: The will of man is by his reason sway'd; And reason says you are the worthier maid.

Culman, 3: Rationi obtempera (Obey reason).

Cf. Tilley, *Prov. in Eng.*, R43.

248   TO **REMEMBER** (REVEAL) A MISFORTUNE (GRIEF) IS TO RENEW IT

Com. of Errors, I, i, 31–32: A heavier task could not have been impos'd Than I to speak my griefs unspeakable. ¶*Othello*, I, iii, 204–205: To mourn a mischief that is past and gone Is the next way to draw new mischief on. ¶*Tempest*, V, i, 199–200: Let us not burthen our remembrance with A heaviness that's gone. ¶*Winter's T.*, V, i, 119–120: No more! cease! Thou know'st He dies to me again when talk'd of.

Publilius Syrus (1934), 545: Post calamitatem memoria alia est calamitas (After misfortune, remembrance is misfortune renewed).

Cf. Tilley, *Eliz. Prov. Lore*, 515, *Prov. in Eng.*, R89.

249   THE **REMEMBRANCE** OF PAST PERILS
            (LOSSES, WOES) IS PLEASANT

Rom. & Jul., III, v, 52–53: All these woes shall serve For sweet discourses in our time to come. ¶*All's Well*, V, iii, 19–20: Praising what is lost Makes the remembrance dear.

Publilius Syrus (1835), 212: Dulcis malorum praeteritorum memoria (Pleasant is the remembrance of the ills that are past).

Cicero, *De Fin.*, ii, 32, 105: Iucunda memoria est praeteritorum malorum (The memory of past evils is pleasant). ¶Seneca, *Hercules Furens*, 656–657: Quae fuit durum pati, meminisse dulce est (What was hard to bear, it is pleasant to recall). ¶Statius, *Thebaidos*, v, 48: Dulce loqui miseris veteresque reducere questus (It is pleasant to the unhappy to speak and to recall the sorrows of old time). ¶Erasmus, *Adagia*, 1149F: Jucunda malorum praeteritorum memoria (The memory of past evils is pleasant).

Cf. Tilley, *Eliz. Prov. Lore*, 516, *Prov. in Eng.*, R73.

250   IN SORROW (CALAMITY, MISERY)
            REPROACH IS CRUEL

Titus Andr., III, i, 246: Sorrow flouted at is double death.

Culman, 5: Calamitas nemini exprobranda (His misery is to be upbraided to no man). ¶*Ibid.*, 7: Infelicitas nemini objicienda (Misfortune is to be objected to nobody). ¶*Ibid.*, 12: Exprobratio calamitatis nemini objicienda (No man must be upbraided with his calamity). ¶* Publilius Syrus (1934), 101: Crudelis est in re adversa obiurgatio

(Rebuke is cruel in adversity). ¶*Ibid.*, 486: Obiurgari in calamitate gravius est quam calamitas (To be scolded in misfortune is harder than misfortune's self).

251   THE HOPE OF **REWARD** IS THE SOLACE OF LABOR

Hen. V, II, ii, 37: Labour shall refresh itself with hope.

Publilius Syrus (1835), 244: Ex praemi spe laboris fit solatium (The hope of reward is the solace of labor).

252   THE **RICH** HAVE MANY FRIENDS

Pass. Pilgr., 20, 35–36: Every man will be thy friend Whilst thou hast wherewith to spend. ¶*Hamlet*, III, ii, 217: Who not needs shall never lack a friend. ¶*Timon*, IV, iii, 311–314: What man didst thou ever know unthrift that was beloved after his means [were gone]? —Who, without those means thou talk'st of, didst thou ever know belov'd?

Culman, 5: Amicos pecuniae faciunt (Monies do make friends). ¶*Ibid.*, 14: Opes amicos conciliant (Wealth procureth friends).

Erasmus, *Adagia*, 829D: Felicitas multos habet amicos (Good fortune has many friends).

Cf. Tilley, *Prov. in Eng.*, R103.

253   **RICHES** BRING ON CARE AND MISERY

Timon, IV, ii, 31–32: Who would not wish to be from wealth exempt, Since riches point to misery and contempt?

Publilius Syrus (1835), 854: Res inquieta est in se ipsam felicitas (Prosperity is ever providing itself with anxieties).

Horace, *Odes*, iii, 16, 17–18: Crescentem sequitur cura pecuniam maiorumque fames (As money grows, care and greed for greater riches follow after).

Cf. Tilley, *Prov. in Eng.*, R109.

254 GOOD **RIDING** AT TWO ANCHORS MEN HAVE
BEEN TOLD, FOR IF THE ONE FAIL
THE OTHER MAY HOLD

Twelfth N., I, v, 24–26: Not so, neither; but I am resolv'd on two points. —That if one break, the other will hold.

Publilius Syrus (1835), 122: Bonum est, duabus anchoris niti ratem (It is well to moor your bark with two anchors).

Erasmus, *Adagia*, 1139D: Bonum est duabus niti ancoris (It is well to moor with two anchors).

Cf. Tilley, *Eliz. Prov. Lore*, 7, *Prov. in Eng.*, R119.

255 AN EXTREME **RIGHT** IS AN EXTREME
WRONG

Rich. II, V, iii, 64: Overflow of good converts to bad. ¶ *Hamlet*, IV, vii, 118–119: For goodness, growing to a plurisy, Dies in his own toomuch.

Publilius Syrus (1835), 939: Summum jus summa plerumque est injuria (An ultra right is generally an ultra wrong).

Cicero, *De Offic.*, i, 10, 33: Summum ius summa iniuria (More law, less justice). ¶ Erasmus, *Adagia*, 374D: Summum jus, summa injuria (An ultra right is an ultra wrong).

Cf. Taverner, 26; Bacon, *Promus*, 54, 1002; Tilley, *Eliz. Prov. Lore*, 200, *Prov. in Eng.*, R122; Smith, 183.

256 THE **RISING** OF ONE MAN IS THE FALLING
OF ANOTHER

Cf. no. 132: One man's gain is another man's loss

K. John, III, iv, 139–140: That John may stand, then Arthur needs must fall. So be it, for it cannot be but so. ¶ *Rich. II*, IV, i, 317–318: Conveyers are you all, That rise thus nimbly by a true king's fall. ¶ *K. Lear*, III, iii, 26: The younger rises when the old doth fall.

* Publilius Syrus (1934), 62: Bona nemini hora est ut non alicui sit mala (Nobody has a good time without its being bad for someone).

Erasmus, *Adagia*, 1055C: Bona nemini hora est, quin alicui sit mala (One man's happy hour is but another's bitter time of trial).

Cf. Tilley, *Eliz. Prov. Lore*, 738, *Prov. in Eng.*, R136.

257   A CHATTY **ROAD-MATE** MAKES SHORT MILES

Lucrece, 791: Palmers' chat makes short their pilgrimage. ¶ *Rich. II*, II, iii, 6–12: Your fair discourse . . . hath very much beguil'd The tediousness and process of my travel.

* Publilius Syrus (1934), 116: Comes facundus in via pro vehiculo est (A chatty road-mate is as good as a carriage).

Erasmus, *Colloquia Fam.*, 733B: Ut in vehiculo quoque jucundus comes pro vehiculo sit (For good company in a journey does the office of a coach). (II, 76).

Cf. Bacon, *Promus*, 1015; Tilley, *Eliz. Prov. Lore*, 110, *Prov. in Eng.*, C566.

258   **RULE** YOUR TONGUE

L. Lab. Lost, V, ii, 662: Rein thy tongue.

Culman, 2: Linguam tempera (Rule thy tongue). ¶ *Ibid.*, 26: Summa cura lingua regi debet (The tongue must be ruled with a great deal of care).

Plautus, *Rudens*, 1254: Linguae tempera (Control your tongue)! ¶ Cato, *Disticha*, i, 3: Virtutem primam esse puto, compescere linguam (To rule the tongue I reckon virtue's height).

259   BEST **SAFETY** LIES IN FEAR

Hamlet, I, iii, 43: Best safety lies in fear. ¶ *All's Well*, I, i, 214–217: You go so much backward when you fight. —That's for advantage. —So is running away when fear proposes the safety.

* Publilius Syrus (1934), 3: Animus vereri qui scit, scit tuto ingredi (Courage that can fear can take the road with safety). ¶ *Ibid.*, 400: Metuendum est semper, esse cum tutus velis (You must always fear when you would be safe).

260   **SATIETY** ATTENDS ON ABUNDANCE,
HUNGER ATTENDS ON POVERTY

Cf. no. 281: All surfeiting results in disgust

Merch. of V., I, ii, 6–7: They are as sick that surfeit with too much as they that starve with nothing.

Publilius Syrus (1835), 656: Parvo fames constat, magno fastidium (Hunger goes with stinted supplies, disgust attends on abundance).

261   A **SCAR** WHICH BRAVERY BEGETS
IS A BADGE OF HONOR

All's Well, IV, v, 105–106: A scar nobly got, or a noble scar, is a good liv'ry of honour.

Publilius Syrus (1934), 433: Non turpis est cicatrix quam virtus parit (Never ugly is the scar which bravery begets).

262   IN A CALM **SEA** ANYONE MAY BE A PILOT

Troilus & Cres., I, iii, 34–37: The sea being smooth, How many shallow bauble boats dare sail Upon her patient breast, making their way With those of nobler bulk! ¶*Coriol.*, IV, i, 6–7: When the sea was calm, all boats alike Show'd mastership in floating.

Publilius Syrus (1835), 364: In tranquillo esse quisque gubernator potest (Anyone can hold the helm, when the sea is calm).

Seneca, *Epist.*, lxxxv, 34: Tranquillo enim, ut aiunt, quilibet gubernator est (For anyone, in the words of the proverb, is a pilot on a calm sea). ¶Erasmus, *Adagia*, 1047E: Tranquillo quilibet gubernator est (In tranquility everyone is a pilot).

Cf. Bacon, *Promus*, 431; Tilley, *Prov. in Eng.*, S174.

263   HE THAT IS TOO **SECURE** IS NOT SAFE

Rich. II, II, i, 266: And yet we strike not, but securely perish. ¶*Troilus & Cres.*, II, ii, 14–15: The wound of peace is surety, Surety secure. ¶*K. Lear*, IV, i, 19–21: Full oft 'tis seen Our means secure us, and our mere defects Prove our commodities. ¶ *Macb.*, III, v, 32–33: And you all know security Is mortals' chiefest enemy.

Culman, 13: Innumera mala parit securitas (Security breeds many mischiefs). ¶ Publilius Syrus (1934), 280: Irritare est calamitatem cum te felicem voces (To call yourself "happy" is to provoke disaster).

Cf. Tilley, *Prov. in Eng.*, W152.

264   PAST **SHAME**, PAST AMENDMENT (GRACE)

Cymb., I, i, 131–137: O disloyal thing . . . Past grace? obedience? — Past hope, and in despair; that way, past grace.

Culman, 25: Pudore amisso omnis virtus ruit (When shame is lost, all virtue quickly decays). ¶ * Publilius Syrus (1934), 196: Fidem qui perdit quo rem servat relicuam (With credit lost, what means are there of saving what remains)?

Plautus, *Bacchides*, 487: Nam ego illum periisse dico quoi quidem periit pudor (For perished I say he has, when his sense of shame has perished).

Cf. Tilley, *Prov. in Eng.*, S271.

265   A COMMON **SHIPWRECK** IS A COMFORT
TO ALL

Timon, V, i, 194–196: I love my country and am not One that rejoices in the common wrack, As common bruit doth put it.

Culman, 11: Commune naufragium omnibus solatium (A common shipwreck is a comfort to all). ¶ Publilius Syrus (1835), 148: Commune naufragium omnibus solatio est (Society in shipwreck is a comfort to all).

Erasmus, *Adagia*, 1009C: Commune naufragium, omnibus solatium (A common shipwreck is a consolation to all).

266   **SILENCE** IS WOMAN'S BEST ORNAMENT

Coriol., II, i, 192: But O, thy wife! —My gracious silence, hail!

Culman, 7: Mulierem ornat silentium (Silence adorneth a woman).

Sophocles, *Ajax*, 293: γυναιξὶ κόσμον ἡ σιγὴ φέρει (For women silence is a grace); cf. Aristotle, *Politics*, i, 5, 8. ¶ Erasmus, *Adagia*, 991A: Mulierem ornat silentium (Silence distinguishes a woman). Cf. Taverner, 63; Tilley, *Prov. in Eng.*, S447.

267   BE REPROACHED FOR **SILENCE**,
              NEVER FOR SPEECH

All's Well, I, i, 76–77: Be check'd for silence, But never tax'd for speech. ¶ *Ibid.*, II, iv, 22–23: Why, I say nothing. —Marry, you are the wiser man.

Culman, 19: Eximia est virtus praestare silentia rebus (It is an excellent virtue to be silent in matters). ¶ *Ibid.*, 23: Non ulli tacuisse nocet, nocet esse locutum (It hurts not any man to hold his peace, it hurts to have spoken). ¶ *Ibid.*, 27: Silendo nemo peccat, loquendo persaepe (No man offends by being silent, but very often by speaking). ¶ Publilius Syrus (1835), 1089: Saepius locutum, nunquam me tacuisse poenitet (I have often regretted my speech, never my silence).

Cato, *Disticha*, i, 12: Nulli tacuisse nocet, nocet esse locutum (To be silent never did harm; it is speech that is harmful). ¶ Plutarch, *Moralia*: *Ed. of Children*, 10F: αὖ σιωπήσας μὲν οὐδεὶς μετενόησε, λαλήσαντες δὲ παμπληθεῖς (Nobody was ever sorry because he kept silent, but hundreds because they talked). ¶ *Ibid.*: On *Garrulity*, 515A: τὸ Σιμωνίδειον ὅτι λαλήσας μὲν πολλάκις μετενόησε, σιωπήσας δ' οὐδέποτε (The saying of Simonides, that he had often repented of speaking, but never of holding his tongue). Cf. Stevenson, 2113:16.

268   WE ARE ALL **SINNERS**

2 Hen. VI, III, iii, 31: We are sinners all.

Culman, 34: Nemo sine peccato est (No man is without sin). ¶ *Ibid.*: Omnes sumus peccatores (We are all sinners).

Seneca, *De Ira*, ii, 28, 1: Nobis persuadeamus, neminem nostrum esse sine culpa (Let us convince ourselves that no one of us is free from fault). Cf. Stevenson, 2116:11.

269   SLANDER ALWAYS SHOOTS AT VIRTUE

Hamlet, I, iii, 38: Virtue itself scapes not calumnious strokes. ¶ *Ibid.*, III, i, 140–142: Be thou as chaste as ice, as pure as snow, thou shalt not escape calumny. ¶ *Meas. for Meas.*, III, ii, 197–198: Back-wounding calumny The whitest virtue strikes. ¶ *Winter's T.*, II, i, 73–74: Calumny will sear Virtue itself.

Culman, 27: Semper malis invisa fuit egregia virtus (Excellent virtue was ever looked maliciously at by wicked men).

Cf. Tilley, *Prov. in Eng.*, E175.

270   SLANDER IS MORE INJURIOUS
THAN OPEN VIOLENCE

Cf. no. 341: Words cut deeper than swords

Cymb., III, iv, 35–36: 'Tis slander, Whose edge is sharper than the sword. ¶ *Winter's T.*, II, iii, 85–86: Slander, Whose sting is sharper than the sword's.

Publilius Syrus (1835), 386: Injuriae plus in maledicto est quam in manu (Slander is more injurious than open violence). ¶ *Ibid.*, 695: Plus in maledicto quam in manu est injuriae (Slander is a greater outrage than personal violence).

271   SLEEP IS THE IMAGE OF DEATH

Lucrece, 402–404: The map of death, And death's dim look in life's mortality. Each in her sleep themselves so beautify. ¶ *Mids. Night's D.*, III, ii, 364–365: Till o'er their brows death-counterfeiting sleep ... doth creep. ¶ *Macb.*, II, ii, 53–54: The sleeping and the dead Are but as pictures. ¶ *Ibid.*, iii, 81: Downy sleep, death's counterfeit. ¶ *Cymb.*, II, ii, 31: O sleep, thou ape of death. ¶ *Winter's T.*, V, iii, 18–20: Prepare To see the life as lively mock'd as ever Still sleep mock'd death.

Culman, 9: Somnus mortis imago (Sleep is the image of death).

Homer, *Iliad*, xiv, 231: ενθ' Ὕπνῳ ξύμβλητο, κασιγνήτῳ Θανάτοιο (There she met Sleep, the brother of Death). ¶ Cato, *Collectio Monos.*,

19: Mortis imago iuvat somnus (Death's copy, sleep, delights). ¶ Vergil, *Aeneid*, vi, 522: Dulcis et alta quies placidaeque simillima morti (Sleep sweet and deep, very image of death's peace). ¶ Ovid, *Amores*, ii, 9, 41: Quid est somnus, gelidae nisi mortis imago (What else is sleep but the image of chill death)?

Cf. Anders, 49; Baldwin, I, 591; Smith, 596; Stevenson, 2137:9; Tilley, *Prov. in Eng.*, S527.

272   THERE IS POOR **SLEEPING** WITH CARE (FEAR) FOR A BEDFELLOW

Rom. & Jul., II, iii, 36: Where care lodges sleep will never lie.

* Publilius Syrus (1934), 359: Metus cum venit, rarum habet somnus locum (When fear has come, sleep has scanty place).

273   **SPARE** THE MAN, CONDEMN HIS VICES

Hen. V, II, ii, 165: My fault, but not my body, pardon, sovereign. ¶ *Meas. for Meas.*, II, ii, 37: Condemn the fault, and not the actor.

Publilius Syrus (1835), 648: Pacem cum hominibus, bellum cum vitiis habe (Be at peace with men, be at war with their vices). ¶ *Ibid.*, 1086: Res bona est, non extirpare sceleratos, sed scelera (Not the criminals, but their crimes, it is well to extirpate).

Martial, *Epigr.*, x, 33, 10: Parcere personis, dicere de vitiis (To spare the person, to denounce the offense). ¶ Erasmus, *Enchiridion*, 64C: Irascere vitio, non homini (Be angry with the vice, not with the man).

Cf. Tilley, *Eliz. Prov. Lore*, 659, *Prov. in Eng.*, P238.

274   A LITTLE **SPARK** NEGLECTED MAY KINDLE A GREAT FIRE

3 Hen. VI, IV, viii, 7–8: A little fire is quickly trodden out, Which, being suffer'd, rivers cannot quench.

Culman, 24: Parva scintilla contempta maximum excitat incendium (A little spark being neglected hath caused a very great fire).

Horace, *Epist.*, i, 18, 85 : Neglecta solent incendia sumere vires (Fires neglected are wont to gather strength). ¶ Quintus Curtius, *Hist. Alex. Magni*, vi, 3, 11 : Parva saepe scintilla contempta magnum excitavit incendium (Often to have ignored a tiny spark has roused a great conflagration). ¶ Erasmus, *Adagia*, 911F : Ex minutissima scintillula gravissimum incendium (From the smallest spark comes the greatest fire).

Cf. Stevenson, 806:9; Tilley, *Prov. in Eng.*, S714.

275   TO **SPEAK** AS ONE THINKS

2 Hen. VI, III, i, 247 : Say as you think and speak it from your souls. ¶ *1 Hen. VI*, V, iii, 141 : Speaks Suffolk as he thinks ? ¶ *Mids. Night's D.*, III, ii, 191 : You speak not as you think. ¶ *Much Ado*, I, i, 226 : I speak my thought. ¶ *Ibid.*, III, ii, 14 : What his heart thinks, his tongue speaks. ¶ *As You Like It*, III, ii, 264 : When I think, I must speak. ¶ *Hamlet*, III, ii, 196 : I do believe you think what now you speak. ¶ *Coriol.*, III, i, 258 : What his breast forges, that his tongue must vent.

* Publilius Syrus (1835), 325 : Homo semper in os fert aliud, aliud cogitat (It is easy for men to say one thing, and think another).

Erasmus, *Adagia*, 381B : Ex animo loqui (To speak from one's mind).

Cf. Bacon, *Promus*, 5 ; Tilley, *Prov. in Eng.*, H334, S725.

276   WHAT IT IS DISGRACEFUL TO DO,
        IT IS HARMFUL TO **SPEAK** OF

K. John, III, i, 38–41 : What other harm have I, good lady, done But spoke the harm that is by others done ? —Which harm within itself so heinous is As it makes harmful all that speak of it.

Culman, 12 : Gravis culpa, tacenda loqui (It is a grievous fault to speak things that are not to be spoken). ¶ Publilius Syrus (1835), 812 : Quod facere turpe est, dicere honestum ne puta (What it is disgraceful to do, think it no honor to speak of).

277 **SPEECH** IS A CURE FOR SORROW

Cf. no. 144: Mute grief feels a keener pang than that which cries aloud; no. 227: Pain (Grief, Love) that has no voice amid torture is a hell *Venus & A.*, 333–334: Of concealed sorrow may be said: Free vent of words love's fire doth assuage. ¶*Lucrece*, 1330: Sorrow ebbs, being blown with wind of words. ¶*L. Lab. Lost*, V, ii, 762: Honest plain words best pierce the ear of grief. ¶*Rich. III*, IV, iv, 126–131: Words? —Windy attorneys to their client woes ... Let them have scope ... they ease the heart. ¶*All's Well*, III, iv, 42: Grief would have tears, and sorrow bids me speak.

Culman, 9: Sermo medetur tristitiae (The speech doth cure sorrow). ¶*Ibid.*, 24: Placidis dictis dolor recte curabitur (Grief will be well eased with sweet words).

278 AFTER A **STORM** COMES A CALM

Othello, II, i, 187: After every tempest come such calms.

Culman, 16: Sequitur facile tempestatem serenitas (A calm doth easily follow a storm).

Cf. Tilley, *Eliz. Prov. Lore*, 591, *Prov. in Eng.*, S908.

279 **STRIKE** WHILE THE IRON IS HOT

3 Hen. VI, V, i, 49: Strike now, or else the iron cools ¶*Hen. VIII*, V, i, 175–176: Now, While It is hot, I'll put it to the issue.

Publilius Syrus (1835), 265: Ferrum, dum in igni candet, cudendum est tibi (You should hammer your iron when it is glowing hot).

Cf. Tilley, *Prov. in Eng.*, I94.

280 MANY **STROKES** FELL GREAT OAKS

3 Hen. VI, II, i, 54–55: Many strokes, though with a little axe, Hews down and fells the hardest-timber'd oak.

Culman, 13: Multis ictibus dejicitur quercus (An oak is hewn down with many blows).

Erasmus, *Adagia*, 331E: Multis ictibus dejicitur quercus (An oak is felled by many strokes).

Cf. Tilley, *Prov. in Eng.*, S941.

281   ALL **SURFEITING** RESULTS IN DISGUST

Cf. no. 260: Satiety attends on abundance, hunger attends on poverty

Mids. Night's D., II, ii, 137–138: A surfeit of the sweetest things The deepest loathing to the stomach brings. ¶*1 Hen. IV*, III, ii, 71–72: They surfeited with honey and began To loathe the taste of sweetness. ¶*Meas. for Meas.*, I, ii, 130: Surfeit is the father of much fast.

Publilius Syrus (1835), 614: Nulla est voluptas, quin assiduae taedeat (There is no pleasure which continued enjoyment cannot render disgusting).

Seneca, *Epist.*, xxiii, 6: In praecipiti voluptas ad dolorem vergit, nisi modum tenuit (Pleasure, unless it has been kept within bounds, tends to rush headlong into the abyss of sorrow).

Cf. Tilley, *Prov. in Eng.*, S1011.

282   **SWEAR** NOT

L. Lab. Lost, V, ii, 841: Swear not, lest ye be forsworn again. ¶*Rom. & Jul.*, II, ii, 109: Swear not by the moon. ¶*Ibid.*, 112: Do not swear at all. ¶*Ibid.*, 116: Well, do not swear. ¶*Rich. III*, IV, iv, 395: Swear not by time to come. ¶*Much Ado*, IV, i, 277: Do not swear. ¶*Jul. Caesar*, II, i, 114: Not an oath. ¶*Twelfth N.*, V, i, 173: O, do not swear! ¶*K. Lear*, III, iv, 82: Swear not. ¶*Cymb.*, II, iv, 143: No swearing. ¶*Winter's T.*, V, ii, 171: You may say it, but not swear it. ¶*Tempest*, V, i, 123: I'll not swear.

Culman, 2: Ne jurato (Swear not).

283   IT IS UNBECOMING TO **TEACH** YOUR
MASTER (TEACHER)

L. Lab. Lost, II, i, 108: To teach a teacher ill beseemeth me.

Publilius Syrus (1835), 479: Malum est habere servum, qui dominum docet (He is a bad servant who teaches his master).

284   THE THINGS WHICH HURT US TEACH US

Cf. no. 20: Calamity (Extremity) stirs up the wit

K. Lear, II, iv, 305–307: To wilful men The injuries that they them-selves procure Must be their schoolmasters. ¶*Timon*, III, v, 45–51: If there be Such valour in the bearing, . . . the felon Loaden with irons wiser than the judge, If wisdom be in suffering.

Culman, 9: Quae nocent docent (The things which hurt us do teach us). ¶*Ibid.*, 12: Eruditiores efficimur omnes damno (We are all made wiser by loss).

Erasmus, *Adagia*, 39E: Quae nocent, docent (The things that are harmful teach).

285   TEARS GRATIFY A SAVAGE NATURE

Lucrece, 558–560: His heart granteth No penetrable entrance to her plaining. Tears harden lust.

Publilius Syrus (1934), 128: Crudelis lacrimis pascitur non frangitur (Cruelty is fed, not broken, by tears).

286   THEY THAT THINK NO ILL ARE
SOONEST BEGUILED

Hamlet, IV, vii, 135–140: He, being remiss, Most generous, and free from all contriving, Will not peruse the foils; so that . . . you may choose A sword unbated, and, in a pass of practice, Requite him for your father. ¶*Othello*, I, iii, 405–408: The Moor is of a free and open nature That thinks men honest that but seem to be so; And will as tenderly be led by th' nose As asses are. ¶*K. Lear*, I, ii, 195–197: A brother noble, Whose nature is so far from doing harms That he suspects none.

Publilius Syrus (1835), 577: Nimia simplicitas facile deprimitur dolis (Too much candor is easily duped).

Cf. Tilley, *Prov. in Eng.*, T221.

287   TIME BRINGS FORTH MANY THINGS

Othello, I, iii, 377–378: There are many events in the womb of time, which will be delivered.

Culman, 5: Dies affert multa (Time brings many things about). ¶ *Ibid.*, 8: Omnia fert aetas (Time affords all things).

288   TIME BRINGS THE TRUTH TO LIGHT

Lucrece, 939–940: Time's glory is . . . To unmask falsehood and bring truth to light.

Culman, 27: Tempus ad lucem ducit veritatem (Time brings the truth to light).

Erasmus, *Adagia*, 528B: Veritatem tempus in lucem eruit (Time brings the truth to light).

Cf. Tilley, *Prov. in Eng.*, T324.

289   TIME CURES ALL THINGS

3 Hen. VI, III, iii, 76–77: For though usurpers sway the rule awhile, Yet heav'ns are just and time suppresseth wrongs. ¶ *Cymb.*, III, v, 37–38: The cure whereof, my lord, 'Tis time must do.

Publilius Syrus (1934), 467: Nihil non aut lenit aut domat diuturnitas (There's naught that time does not either soothe or quell).

Euripides, *Alcestis*, 1085: χρόνος μαλάξει (Time will bring healing). ¶ Menander, *Frag.*, 677K: πάντων ἰατρὸς τῶν ἀναγκαίων κακῶν χρόνος ἐστίν (Time is healer of all the necessary ills). ¶ Seneca, *Ad Marciam de Con.*, i, 6: Naturale remedium temporis (Nature's great healer, time).

Cf. Stevenson, 2329: 2–7; Tilley, *Prov. in Eng.*, T325.

290   TIME DEVOURS ALL THINGS

L. Lab. Lost, I, i, 4: Spite of cormorant devouring Time. ¶ *Sonnets*, 19, 1: Devouring Time, blunt thou the lion's paws.

Culman, 9: Tempus edax rerum (Time is a devourer of things).

Cato, *Collectio Monos.*, 67: Omne manu factum consumit longa vetustas (Long lapse of time consumes all handiwork). ¶Ovid, *Metam.*, xv, 234: Tempus edax rerum (Time is the devourer of things).
Cf. Stevenson, 2327:5; Tilley, *Prov. in Eng.*, T326.

291   TIME (LIFE) IS LONG TO THE WRETCHED,
SHORT TO THE HAPPY

Rich. II, I, iii, 260–261: Six winters . . . are quickly gone. —To men in joy; but grief makes one hour ten. ¶*Othello*, II, iii, 385: Pleasure and action make the hours seem short.
    * Publilius Syrus (1934), 485: O vita misero longa, felici brevis (How long life is to the wretched, how short to the happy)!

292   TIME IS SWIFT-FOOTED

Two Gent., I, iii, 23: The swift course of time. ¶*Sonnets*, 19, 6: Do whate'er thou wilt, swift-footed Time.
    Culman, 8: Nihil fugacius tempore (Nothing is more fleeting than time). ¶*Ibid.*, 9: Tempus celerrime aufugit (Time runs away very swiftly). ¶*Ibid.*: Tempore nihil velocius (Nothing is swifter than time).
    Vergil, *Georgics*, iii, 284: Sed fugit interea, fugit inreparabile tempus (Time is flying, flying beyond recall).
    Cf. Bacon, *Promus*, 422; Stevenson, 2322–2323; Tilley, *Prov. in Eng.*, T327.

293   TIME IS THE NURSE AND BREEDER
OF ALL GOOD

Two Gent., III, i, 243: Time is the nurse and breeder of all good.
    Publilius Syrus (1835), 795: Quicquid futurum egregium est, sero absolvitur (It takes a long time to bring excellence to maturity).

294   TIME PUTS AN END TO LOVE

Hamlet, IV, vii, 112–114: Love is begun by time, And that I see, in passages of proof, Time qualifies the spark and fire of it. ¶ *Cymb.*, II, iii, 47–49: She hath not yet forgot him. Some more time Must wear the print of his remembrance out, And then she's yours.

Publilius Syrus (1934), 42: Amori finem tempus, non animus, facit ('Tis time, not the mind, that puts an end to love).

Ovid, *Rem. Amoris*, 503: Intrat amor mentes usu, dediscitur usu (By wont love comes into the mind, by wont is love unlearnt).

Cf. Tilley, *Eliz. Prov. Lore*, 633, *Prov. in Eng.*, T340.

295   TIME REVEALS ALL THINGS

Twelfth N., II, ii, 41–42: O Time, thou must untangle this, not I; It is too hard a knot for me t' untie! ¶ *K. Lear*, I, i, 283: Time shall unfold what plighted cunning hides.

Culman, 9: Tempus omnia revelat (Time reveals all things).

Erasmus, *Adagia*, 527F: Tempus omnia revelat (Time reveals all things).

Cf. Taverner, 35; Tilley, *Prov. in Eng.*, T333.

296   TIME TAKES AWAY GRIEF

Two Gent., III, ii, 15: A little time, my lord, will kill that grief.

Culman, 5: Dies aegritudinem adimit (Time takes away grief). ¶ *Ibid.*: Doloris medicus tempus (Time is the physician of grief). ¶ *Ibid.*, 9: Tempus dolorem lenit (Time doth assuage grief).

Terence, *Heauton*, 421–422: Illud falsumst quod volgo audio dici, diem adimere aegritudinem hominibus (There is no truth in the saying I so often hear that time removes distress). ¶ Quintilian, *Inst. Orat.*, vi, 1, 28: Etiam veros dolores mitiget tempus (Time assuages even genuine grief). ¶ Erasmus, *Adagia*, 556B: Dies adimit aegritudinem (A day takes away grief).

Cf. Anders, 47; Baldwin, I, 591; Tilley, *Prov. in Eng.*, T322.

297   COMPLY WITH THE TIME

L. Lab. Lost, V, ii, 63: Wait the season, and observe the times. ❡*Othello*,
I, iii, 301: We must obey the time.
 Culman, 3: Tempori pare (Observe the time).
 Cicero, *De Fin.*, iii, 22, 73: Tempori parere (Obey the occasion).
❡Erasmus, *Adagia*, 460C: Tempori parere (Comply with the time).

298   THERE'S A TIME FOR ALL THINGS

Com. of Errors, II, ii, 66: There's a time for all things. ❡*Ibid.*, 101–102:
You would all this time have prov'd there is no time for all
things.
 Culman, 14: Omnia suo tempore peragenda (All things are to be
done in their own time).
 Cf. Tilley, *Prov. in Eng.*, T314.

299   TODAY IS THE PUPIL OF YESTERDAY

Hen. VIII, I, i, 16–17: Each following day Became the next day's
master.
 * Publilius Syrus (1934), 146: Discipulus est prioris posterior dies
(Next day is pupil of the day before).
 Cf. Smith, 662.

**300   WHERE YOUR TREASURE IS, THERE
            YOUR HEART IS ALSO**

2 Hen. VI, II, i, 19–20: Thy heaven is on earth; thine eyes and thoughts
Beat on a crown, the treasure of thy heart.
 Culman, 28: Ubi quisque thesaurum habet, ibi habet & cor (Where
everyone hath his treasure, there also he hath his heart).
 New Testament: Matthew, vi, 21: ὅπου γάρ ἐστιν ὁ θησαυρός σου, ἐκεῖ

ἔσται ἡ καρδία σου (For where your treasure is, there will your heart be also).

Cf. Stevenson, 2367:11; Tilley, *Prov. in Eng.*, T485.

301   A **TREE** IS KNOWN BY ITS FRUIT

1 Hen. IV, II, iv, 470–471: The tree may be known by the fruit, as the fruit by the tree.

Culman, 28: Arbor ex fructibus cognoscitur (A tree is known by its fruit).

New Testament: *Matthew*, xii, 33: ἐκ γὰρ τοῦ καρποῦ τὸ δένδρον γινώσκεται (For the tree is known by its fruit). ❡ Erasmus, *Adagia*, 348C: De fructu arborem cognosco (I know a tree by its fruit).

Cf. Tilley, *Eliz. Prov. Lore*, 642, *Prov. in Eng.*, T497; Baldwin, I, 591–592; Stevenson, 2370:9.

302   **TRUST** NO MAN

2 Hen. VI, IV, iv, 58: Trust nobody, for fear you be betray'd. ❡ *Hen. V*, II, iii, 52–53: Trust none; For oaths are straws, men's faiths are wafer-cakes. ❡ *Timon*, I, ii, 64–66: I pray . . . I may never prove so fond To trust man on his oath or bond.

Culman, 30: Confidendum non est in homine (We must not trust in man). ❡ *Ibid.*, 32: Homini non fidendum (We must not trust in man).

303   PLAIN **TRUTH** SHOWS UP BEST

Cf. no. 304: The language of truth is simple

1 Hen. VI, II, iv, 20–21: The truth appears so naked on my side That any purblind eye may find it out. ❡ *Rich. III*, IV, iv, 358: An honest tale speeds best being plainly told. ❡ *Timon*, V, i, 67–70: I am rapt, and cannot cover The monstrous bulk of this ingratitude With any size of words. —Let it go naked; men may see't the better.

Culman, 14: Nihil efficacius simplici veritate (Nothing is more effectual than plain truth).

Cf. Tilley, *Prov. in Eng.*, T589.

304   THE LANGUAGE OF TRUTH IS SIMPLE

Cf. no. 303: Plain truth shows up best

L. Lab. Lost, V, ii, 412–413: Henceforth my wooing mind shall be express'd In russet yea's and honest kersey no's. ¶ *Mids.Night's D.*, V, i, 129: Wonder on, till truth make all things plain. ¶ *All's Well*, IV, ii, 21–22: 'Tis not the many oaths that makes the truth, But the plain single vow that is vow'd true.

Culman, 10: Veritatis simplex oratio (The speech of truth is plain). Aeschylus, *Frag.*, 92: ἁπλᾶ γάρ ἐστι τῆς ἀληθείας ἔπη (Simple are the words of truth). ¶ Euripides, *Phoenissae*, 469: ἁπλοῦς ὁ μῦθος τῆς ἀληθείας ἔφυ (Plain and unvarnished are the words of truth). ¶ Cato, *Disticha*, iii, 4: Simplicitas veri forma est (Truth is naked). ¶ Seneca, *Epist.*, xlix, 12: Veritatis simplex oratio est (The language of truth is simple). ¶ Marcellinus, *Res Gestae*, xiv, 10, 13: Veritatis enim absolutio semper est simplex (For perfect truth is always simple). ¶ Erasmus, *Adagia*, 145 F: Veritatis simplex oratio (The language of truth is simple).

Cf. Taverner, 14; Stevenson, 2384:7; Tilley, *Prov. in Eng.*, T593.

305   WHEN YOU SEEK THE TRUTH, SPEAK FREELY

Hen. VIII, III, i, 39: Out with it boldly. Truth loves open dealing.

Publilius Syrus (1934), 348: Licentiam des linguae cum verum petas (You must give licence to the tongue when you ask for the truth).

306   TRY YOUR FRIEND BEFORE YOU TRUST HIM

Hamlet, I, iii, 62–63: Those friends thou hast, and their adoption tried, Grapple them unto thy soul with hoops of steel.

Culman, 1: Amicos probato (Try thy friends). ¶ Publilius Syrus (1934), 134: Cave amicum credas nisi si quem probaveris (Mind you think no man a friend save him you have tried).

Cicero, *De Amic.*, xxii, 85: Cum iudicaris, diligere oportet (You should love your friend after you have appraised him). ¶ Seneca, *Epist.*, iii, 2: Post amicitiam credendum est, ante amicitiam iudicandum (When friendship is settled, you must trust; before friendship is formed, you must pass judgment).

Cf. Udall, *Apoph. of Erasm.*, 68:47; Tilley, *Eliz. Prov. Lore*, 651, *Prov. in Eng.*, T595.

307   ONE GOOD TURN BEGETS (ASKS, REQUIRES, DESERVES) ANOTHER

Hamlet, IV, vi, 20–22: They have dealt with me like thieves of mercy; but they knew what they did: I am to do a good turn for them. ¶*Twelfth N.*, III, iii, 15–18: Oft good turns Are shuffled off with such uncurrent pay. But, were my worth as is my conscience firm, You should find better dealing. ¶*Meas. for Meas.*, IV, ii, 61–62: Truly, sir, for your kindness I owe you a good turn. ¶*Timon*, III, ii, 67: I'll look you out a good turn [for this favor to me]. ¶*Ant. & Cleop.*, II, v, 58–59: He's bound unto Octavia. —For what good turn? —For the best turn i' th' bed. ¶*Sonnets*, 24, 9: Now see what good turns eyes for eyes have done. ¶*Ibid.*, 47, 2: And each doth good turns now unto the other.

Culman, 6: Gratia gratiam parit (One good turn begets another). ¶*Ibid.*, 11: Beneficium semper beneficium provocat (One good turn doth always provoke another).

Erasmus, *Adagia*, 40E: Gratia gratiam parit (One good deed brings forth another).

Cf. Tilley, *Prov. in Eng.*, T616.

308   NO MAN CAN DO TWO THINGS AT ONCE

Hamlet, III, iii, 41–43: Like a man to double business bound . . . both neglect.

Culman, 26: Qui simul duplex captat commodum, utroque frustratur (He that catcheth at a double profit at once, is deceived of both). ¶Publilius Syrus (1835), 7: Ad duo festinans neutrum bene peregeris (To do two things at once is to do neither). ¶*Ibid.*, 430: Lepores duo qui insequitur, is neutrum capit (He who chases two hares will catch neither).

Erasmus, *Adagia*, 790A: Duos insequens lepores, neutrum capit (In pursuing two hares a man catches neither).

Cf. Tilley, *Prov. in Eng.*, M318.

309   UNHAPPY HE, WHO CANNOT DO THE GOOD THAT HE WOULD

1 Hen. VI, IV, iii, 43–44: No more my fortune can But curse the cause I cannot aid the man.

Publilius Syrus (1934), 499: Prodesse qui vult nec potest, aeque est miser (The wish to help without the power means sharing misery).

310   IN UNION (CONCORD) THERE IS STRENGTH

Pericles, II, iv, 57–58: You love us, we you, and we'll clasp hands. When peers thus knit, a kingdom ever stands.

* Publilius Syrus (1934), 4: Auxilia humilia firma consensus facit (United feeling makes strength out of humble aids). ¶ *Ibid.*, 327: Ibi semper est victoria ubi concordia est (Victory is ever there where union of hearts is).

Euripides, *Hecuba*, 884: δεινὸν τὸ πλῆθος, σὺν δόλῳ τε δύσμαχον (Mighty are numbers—joined with craft, resistless). ¶ Ovid, *Rem. Amoris*, 420: Quae non prosunt singula, multa iuvant (Things that avail not singly help when they are many).

Cf. Tilley, *Prov. in Eng.*, U11.

311   UNKNOWN (UNSHOWN), UNLOVED

Ant. & Cleop., III, vi, 52–53: Left unshown, Is often left unlov'd.

Culman, 6: Incognitum non amatur (A thing unknown is not desired).

312   A DEED OF **VALOR** IS A DEED OF FAME

Titus Andr., I, i, 390: He lives in fame that died in virtue's cause.
Coriol., II, ii, 88–89: Valour is the chiefest virtue and Most dignifies
the haver.

Publilius Syrus (1934), 590: Quicquid fit cum virtute fit cum gloria
(A deed of valor is a deed of fame).

Cf. Tilley, *Prov. in Eng.*, V74.

313   **VENGEANCE** BELONGS ONLY TO GOD

Rich. II, I, ii, 6–8: Put we our quarrel to the will of heaven, Who, when
they see the hours ripe on earth, Will rain hot vengeance on offenders'
heads.

Publilius Syrus (1934), 702: Unus deus poenam affert, multi cogitant
(God alone brings punishment, though many intend it).

New Testament: *Romans*, xii, 19: ἐμοὶ ἐκδίκησις, ἐγὼ ἀνταποδώσω,
λέγει Κύριος (Vengeance is mine; I will repay, saith the Lord).

Cf. Tilley, *Prov. in Eng.*, V24.

314   WHEN **VICE** IS PROFITABLE,
HE ERRS WHO DOES RIGHT

Macb., IV, ii, 75–77: Where to do harm Is often laudable, to do good
sometime Accounted dangerous folly.

* Publilius Syrus (1934), 113: Cum vitia prosunt, peccat qui recte
facit (When vices pay, the doer of the right is at fault).

315   **VICE** OFTEN HAS A CLOSE RELATIONSHIP
TO VIRTUE

Two Gent., III, i, 324–325: Here follow her vices. —Close at the heels
of her virtues. ¶ *2 Hen. IV*, IV, i, 196: And good from bad find no
partition.

Culman, 14: Mala sunt vicina bonis (Evil things are near to good things). ¶ Publilius Syrus (1835), 983: Vicina saepe vitia sunt virtutibus (Vices often have a close relationship to virtues).

Ovid, *Rem. Amoris*, 323: Mala sunt vicina bonis (Evil things lie near to good things). ¶ Seneca, *Epist.*, cxx, 8: Sunt enim, ut scis, virtutibus vitia confinia (For there are, as you know, vices which are next-door to virtues).

316   VIRTUE (CHASTITY, MODESTY) IS BEAUTY

Twelfth N., III, iv, 401–403: In nature there's no blemish but the mind; None can be call'd deform'd but the unkind. Virtue is beauty. ¶ *Othello*, I, iii, 290–291: If virtue no delighted beauty lack, Your son-in-law is far more fair than black. ¶ *Hamlet*, III, i, 107–108: If you be honest and fair, your honesty should admit no discourse to your beauty.

Culman, 10: Ampla satis forma pudicitia (Modesty is beauty sufficient enough).

Diogenes Laertius, *Zeno*, vii, 23: τὸ κάλλος εἶπε τῆς σωφροσύνης ἄνθος εἶναι (Beauty he called the flower of chastity).

Cf. Tilley, *Prov. in Eng.*, D410.

317   VIRTUE IS THE TRUE NOBILITY

Titus Andr., I, i, 93: Sweet cell of virtue and nobility.

Publilius Syrus (1934), 713: Virum bonum natura non ordo facit (Nature, not rank, makes the gentleman).

Juvenal, *Sat.*, viii, 20: Nobilitas sola est atque unica virtus (Virtue alone is true nobility).

Cf. Tilley, *Eliz. Prov. Lore*, 661, *Prov. in Eng.*, V85.

318   ALL VIRTUE FINDS AN OBSTACLE IN FEAR

Hen. VIII, III, i, 168–169: You wrong your virtues With these weak women's fears.

Publilius Syrus (1934), 728: Virtutis omnis impedimentum est timor (All virtue finds an obstacle in fear).

319 EXERCISE **VIRTUE**

All's Well, V, i, 15–16: I put you to The use of your own virtues.
Culman, 3: Utere virtute (Use vertue).
Cato, *Collectio Dis. Vulg.*, 35: Virtute utere (Practice virtue).

320 EVERYONE SHOULD LABOR IN
HIS OWN **VOCATION**

Cf. no. 19: Everyone as his business lies

2 Hen. VI, IV, ii, 17–18: It is said, 'Labour in thy vocation.' ¶ *1 Hen. IV*, I, ii, 116–117: Why, Hal, 'tis my vocation, Hal. 'Tis no sin for a man to labour in his vocation.

Culman, 26: Quam quisque norit artem, in hac se exerceat (Let every man exercise himself in the art which he knoweth).

Cicero, *Tusc. Disp.*, i, 18, 41: Bene enim illo Graecorum proverbio praecipitur: *Quam quisque norit artem, in hac se exerceat* (For it is a good rule laid down in the well-known Greek saying: "The art which each man knows, in this let him employ himself"). ¶ Erasmus, *Adagia*, 477D: Quam quisque norit artem, in hac se exerceat (One who knows his own profession should work at it).

Cf. Taverner, 31; Tilley, *Prov. in Eng.*, C23.

321 THE CHANCE OF **WAR** IS UNCERTAIN

Titus Andr., I, i, 264: Chance of war hath wrought this change of cheer. ¶ *L. Lab. Lost*, V, ii, 533–534: But we will put it, as they say, to fortuna della guerra. ¶ *1 Hen. IV*, I, iii, 94–95: He never did fall off, my sovereign liege, But by the chance of war. ¶ *2 Hen. IV*, I, i, 166–168: You cast th' event of war . . . And summ'd the accompt of chance before you said, 'Let us make head.' ¶ *Troilus & Cres.*, Prol., 31: Now good or bad, 'tis but the chance of war. ¶ *Coriol.*, V, iii, 141: The end of war's uncertain. ¶ *Cymb.*, V, v, 75–76: Consider, sir, the chance of war. The day Was yours by accident.

Culman, 5 : Belli exitus incertus (The end of war is uncertain). ¶ *Ibid.* :
Belli fortuna anceps (The fortune of war is doubtful).

Cicero, *Pro Milone*, xxi, 56 : Incertos exitus pugnarum (The uncertainty
of the issues of battle). ¶ Cicero, *Epist. Ad Atticum*, vii, 3 : Hic omnia
facere omnes, ne armis decernatur; quorum exitus semper incerti (On
our side we all do everything to avoid battle : you can never be sure of
the issue of war). ¶ Vergil, *Aeneid*, iv, 603 : Anceps pugnae fuerat
fortuna (The issue of battle had been doubtful); cf. xii, 43.

Cf. Bacon, *Promus*, 1101; Anders, 47; Tilley, *Eliz. Prov. Lore*, 664,
Prov. in Eng., C223; Baldwin, I, 591; Stevenson, 2447:2.

322   GOOD **WATCH** PREVENTS MISFORTUNE

Cf. no. 216: Neglect a danger, and it will take you by surprise

1 Hen. VI, II, i, 58–59: Had your watch been good, This sudden
mischief never could have fall'n!

Publilius Syrus (1934), 130: Caret periclo qui etiam cum est tutus
cavet (He's free from danger who even in safety takes precaution).
¶ * *Ibid.* (1835), 61: Aspicere oportet, quicquid nolis perdere (Keep a
sharp watch where you would not lose).

Cf. Tilley, *Prov. in Eng.*, W83.

323   THE GREATEST **WEALTH** IS CONTENTMENT
WITH A LITTLE

Othello, III, iii, 172: Poor and content is rich, and rich enough.

Culman, 18 : Dives est, qui nihil sibi deesse putat (He is a rich man
who thinks he wants nothing). ¶ Publilius Syrus (1835), 807: Quis
plurimum habet? is qui omnium minimum cupit (Who has the greatest
possessions? he who wants least).

Lucretius, *De Rerum Natura*, v, 1118–1119: Divitiae grandes homini
sunt vivere parvo aequo animo (Man's greatest riches is to live on a
little with contented mind).

Cf. Tilley, *Prov. in Eng.*, W194.

324   DO NOT PUT A **WEAPON** IN A
MADMAN'S HAND

2 Hen. VI, III, i, 347: You put sharp weapons in a madman's hands.
  * Publilius Syrus (1934), 184: Eripere telum non dare irato decet
(Anger is rightly robbed of a weapon, not given one).
  Plautus, *Casina*, 629: Eripite isti gladium, quae suist impos animi
(Snatch the sword away from her! She's not in possession of her
senses)! ¶ Seneca, *De Ira*, i, 19, 8: Male irato ferrum committitur (It is
not well to trust an angry man with a sword).
  Cf. Tilley, *Prov. in Eng.*, P669.

325   FOR A TOUGH LOG LOOK FOR
A TOUGH **WEDGE**

Troilus & Cres., I, iii, 316: Blunt wedges rive hard knots.
  Publilius Syrus (1835), 738: Quaerendus cuneus est malus trunco
malo (Look for a tough wedge for a tough log).
  Erasmus, *Adagia*, 70F: Malo nodo malus quaerendus cuneus (One
should seek a tough wedge for a tough log).
  Cf. Taverner, 5; Tilley, *Prov. in Eng.*, P289.

326 THE **WICKEDNESS** OF ONE OFTEN BECOMES
THE CURSE OF ALL

Lucrece, 1483–1489: For one's offence why should so many fall, To
plague a private sin in general? . . . And one man's lust these many
lives confounds. ¶ *Timon*, V, iv, 21–26: We were not all unkind, nor
all deserve The common stroke of war . . . nor . . . That these great
tow'rs, trophies, and schools should fall For private faults in them.
  Culman, 27: Saepe mali malefacta viri populus luit omnis (Ofttimes
all the people suffer for a bad man's ill-doing). ¶ Publilius Syrus (1934),
404: Malitia unius cito fit male dictum omnium (The malice of one soon
becomes the curse of all).

327   WHAT WE DO **WILLINGLY** IS EASY

Macb., II, iii, 55: The labour we delight in physics pain. ❡ *Tempest*, III, i, 29–31: I should do it With much more ease; for my good will is to it, And yours it is against.

Culman, 20: Jugum qui fert volens, leve efficit (He that willingly bears the yoke makes it light).

Cf. Tilley, *Prov. in Eng.*, D407.

328   GOOD **WINE** NEEDS NO BUSH

As You Like It, Epil., 4: Good wine needs no bush.

Publilius Syrus (1835), 985: Vino vendibili suspensa hedera non opus (You need not hang up the ivy branch over the wine that will sell).

Erasmus, *Adagia*, 589C: Vino vendibili suspensa hedera nihil opus (For wine that is salable there is no need of hung-up ivy).

Cf. Taverner, 39; Tilley, *Eliz. Prov. Lore*, 686, *Prov. in Eng.*, W462.

329   EXERCISE **WISDOM**

2 Hen. VI, I, i, 157: Be wise and circumspect. ❡ *Com. of Errors*, IV, iii, 76: Master, be wise! ❡ *Othello*, III, iii, 432: Be wise ❡ *Ibid.*, V, ii, 223: Be wise. ❡ *K. Lear*, I, iv, 240: Make use of . . . good wisdom.

Culman, 3: Prudentiam exerce (Exercise wisdom).

330   **WISE** MEN DO NOT BEMOAN
              THEIR WOES (LOSSES)

3 Hen. VI, V, iv, 1: Wise men ne'er sit and wail their loss. ❡ *Rich. II*, III, ii, 178: Wise men ne'er sit and wail their woes.

Culman, 19: Fortunae incommoda nihil movent sapientem (The discommodities of fortune do not at all trouble a wise man).

Cf. Tilley, *Prov. in Eng.*, M999a.

331   A **WISE** MAN KNOWS THAT HE IS A FOOL

As You Like It, V, i, 35–36: The wise man knows himself to be a fool.
¶ *Twelfth N.*, I, v, 37–38: I that am sure I lack thee [wit] may pass for a wise man.

Publilius Syrus (1934), 451: Non pote non sapere qui se stultum intellegit (He must have wit who understands he is a fool).

Cf. Tilley, *Prov. in Eng.*, M425.

332   A **WISE** (VALIANT) MAN MAKES EVERY COUNTRY HIS OWN

Rich. II, I, iii, 275–276: All places that the eye of heaven visits Are to a wise man ports and happy havens.

Culman, 15: Omne solum forti patria (Every soil is a valiant man's country).

Ovid, *Fasti*, i, 493: Omne solum forti patria est (To a brave man every land is his country). ¶ Seneca, *Ad Helviam de Con.*, ix, 7: Scires omnem locum sapienti viro patriam esse (You know that to the wise man every place is his country).

Cf. Tilley, *Eliz. Prov. Lore*, 120, *Prov. in Eng.*, M426; Stevenson, 426:2.

333   NO ONE IS **WISE** AT ALL TIMES

Cf. no. 98: Everyone has his faults; no. 205: Everyone makes mistakes *Othello*, II, iii, 241: But men are men; the best sometimes forget.

Culman, 14: Omnibus horis nemo sapit (No man is wise at all times).

Pliny, *Nat. Hist.*, vii, 40, 131: Nemo mortalium omnibus horis sapit (No mortal man is wise at all times).   Erasmus, *Adagia*, 532B: Nemo mortalium omnibus horis sapit (No mortal man is wise at all times); *Fam.*, 752F.

Cf. Taverner, 35; Smith, 456; Tilley, *Prov. in Eng.*, M335.

334   THERE IS **WITCHCRAFT** IN FAIR WORDS

2 Hen. VI, I, i, 156–157: Let not his smoothing words Bewitch your hearts. ¶ *Hamlet*, I, v, 43–45: With witchcraft of his wit, with traitorous gifts—O wicked wit and gifts, that have the power So to seduce!

* Publilius Syrus (1934), 251: Habet suum venenum blanda oratio (The wheedling speech contains its special poison).
    Cf. Tilley, *Prov. in Eng.*, W588.

335   **WITS** TOO SOON RIPE SOON DECAY

L. Lab. Lost, II, i, 54: Short-liv'd wits do wither as they grow. ¶*Rich. III*, III, i, 79: So wise so young, they say do never live long. ¶*1 Hen. IV*, III, ii, 61–62: Rash bavin wits, Soon kindled and soon burnt.
    Culman, 15: Praecocia ingenia cito desistunt (Soon ripe wits do soon decay).
    Pliny, *Nat. Hist.*, vii, 51, 171–172: Senilem iuventam praematurae mortis esse signum (Precocious youth is a sign of premature death). ¶Quintilian, *Inst. Orat.*, vi, Pref., 10: Observatum fere est celerius occidere festinatam maturitatem (It is a matter of common observation that those who ripen early die young). ¶Erasmus, *Adagia*, 927F: Mors optima rapit, deterrima relinquit (Death takes the best and leaves the worst).
    Cf. Stevenson, 525:5; Tilley, *Prov. in Eng.*, L384.

336   A **WOMAN** EITHER LOVES OR
HATES TO EXTREMES

Venus & A., 987: Thy weal and woe are both of them extremes. ¶*Much Ado*, V, i, 178–179: If she did not hate him deadly, she would love him dearly. ¶*Hamlet*, III, ii, 177–178: For women's fear and love holds quantity, In neither aught, or in extremity.
    * Publilius Syrus (1934), 6: Aut amat aut odit mulier: nihil est tertium (Woman either loves or hates: there is no third thing).
    Cf. Tilley, *Eliz. Prov. Lore*, 701, *Prov. in Eng.*, W651; Baldwin, I, 604.

337   A **WOMAN** IS ALWAYS WAVERING
AND INCONSTANT

1 Hen. IV, II, iii, 111–112: Constant you are, But yet a woman. ¶*Rich. III*, IV, iv, 431: Relenting fool, and shallow, changing woman! ¶*Hamlet*, I, ii, 146: Frailty, thy name is woman! ¶*Cymb.*, II, v, 30:

They [women] are not constant, but are changing still. ¶*Sonnets*, 20, 4: With shifting change, as is false women's fashion.

Culman, 6: Foeminae sunt inconstantes (Women are unconstant). ¶*Ibid.*, 28: Varia & mutabilis semper foemina (A woman is always wavering and unconstant).

Vergil, *Aeneid*, iv, 569: Varium et mutabile semper femina (A fickle and changeful thing is woman ever). ¶Seneca, *De Rem. Fortui.* (Palmer), 62-63: Nihil tam mobile quam foeminarum voluntas, nihil tam vagum (Nothing is so soon moved as a woman's will, nothing so unstable).

Cf. Bacon, *Promus*, 1085; Anders, 48; Tilley, *Eliz. Prov. Lore*, 704, *Prov. in Eng.*, W674; Baldwin, I, 591.

338   NEVER TRUST A **WOMAN** WHEN SHE WEEPS

Timon, I, ii, 63-67: Immortal gods ... Grant I may never prove so fond To trust ... a harlot for her weeping.

* Publilius Syrus (1934), 153: Didicere flere feminae in mendacium (Woman has learned the use of tears to deceive). ¶*Ibid.*, 384: Muliebris lacrima condimentum est malitiae (A woman's tear is the sauce of mischief).

Cato, *Disticha*, iii, 20: Nam lacrimis struit insidias, cum femina plorat (A weeping woman plots but to waylay).

Cf. Tilley, *Prov. in Eng.*, W638.

339   A **WORD** ONCE SPOKEN CAN (CANNOT) BE CALLED BACK

Meas. for Meas., II, ii, 57-58: Too late? Why, no! I, that do speak a word, May call it back again.

Culman, 20: Facile evolat verbum, tamen nunquam redit (A word doth quickly fly out, yet it never returneth).

Horace, *Ars Poetica*, 390: Nescit vox missa reverti (A word once sent forth can never come back). ¶Horace, *Epist.*, i, 18, 71: Semel emissum volat irrevocabile verbum (A word once spoken flies beyond recall). ¶Plutarch, *Moralia: Ed. of Children*, 10F: ῥηθὲν ἀναλαβεῖν ἀδύνατον

(The spoken word cannot possibly be recalled). ¶Erasmus, *Colloquia Fam.*, 696F: Sed verba simul atque semel evolarint, non revolant (But words, when they are once out, cannot be called in again).

Cf. Tilley, *Eliz. Prov. Lore*, 712, *Prov. in Eng.*, W777; Stevenson, 2597:2.

340   **WORDS** BEFORE BLOWS

Jul. Caesar, V, i, 23–27: Shall we give sign of battle? —No, . . . The generals would have some words . . . —Words before blows. ¶*Ant. & Cleop.*, II, vi, 2–3: We shall talk before we fight. —Most meet That first we come to words.

Culman, 5: Bellum gerendum consilio (War is to be made by counsel).

341   **WORDS** CUT DEEPER THAN SWORDS

Cf. no. 270: Slander is more injurious than open violence

3 Hen. VI, II, i, 96–99: If we should recompt Our baleful news and at each word's deliverance Stab poniards in our flesh till all were told, The words would add more anguish than the wounds. ¶*Ibid.*, V, vi, 26–28: Kill me with thy weapon, not with words! My breast can better brook thy dagger's point Than can my ears that tragic history.

Culman, 24: Plures necat lingua, quam gladius (The tongue kills more than the sword).

Cf. Smith, 729; Tilley, *Prov. in Eng.*, W839.

342   OFTEN ONE CAN BE PERSUADED
             BY SMOOTH **WORDS**

Rich. III, IV, i, 79–80: My woman's heart Grossly grew captive to his honey words.

Culman, 11: Blandis verbis homines exorantur (Men are persuaded by good words).

343   EVEN WHEN THE **WOUND** IS HEALED,
THE SCAR REMAINS

Lucrece, 731–732: Bearing away the wound that nothing healeth, The scar that will despite of cure remain.

Publilius Syrus (1835), 239: Etiam sanato vulnere cicatrix manet (Even when the wound is healed, the scar remains).

Seneca, *De Ira*, i, 16, 7: In sapientis quoque animo, etiam cum vulnus sanatum est, cicatrix manet (Even the wise man's mind will keep its scar long after the wound has healed).

Cf. Tilley, *Prov. in Eng.*, W929.

344   IT IS NOT **WRONG** TO HARM ONE WHO
HAS HARMED YOU

Lucrece, 1692–1693: 'Tis a meritorious fair design To chase injustice with revengeful arms.

Publilius Syrus (1934), 281: Impune pecces in eum qui peccat prior (You may safely offend against him who offends first).

Spenser, *F.Q.*, VI, i, 26, 4–5: It is no blame To punish those, that doe deserue the same.

345 TO FORGET A **WRONG** IS THE BEST REMEDY

Cf. no. 225: It is often better to overlook an injury than to avenge it

Coriol., V, iii, 154–155: Think'st thou it honourable for a noble man Still to remember wrongs?

* Publilius Syrus (1934), 289: Iniuriarum remedium est oblivio (For wrongs the cure lies in forgetfulness). ¶ *Ibid.* (1835), 450: Magnanimo injuriae remedium oblivio est (A noble spirit finds a cure for injustice in forgetting it).

Seneca, *Epist.*, xciv, 28: Iniuriarum remedium est oblivio (Forgetting trouble is the way to cure it).

Cf. Tilley, *Prov. in Eng.*, W946.

346   **YOUTH AND AGE CANNOT AGREE**

L. Lab. Lost, IV, iii, 217: Young blood doth not obey an old decree.
¶ *Pass. Pilgr.*, 12, 1: Crabbed age and youth cannot live together.

Culman, 26: Senex homo est molestus coetui juvenum (An old man is troublesome to young men's company).

Terence, *Hecyra*, 619: Odiosa haec est aetas adulescentulis (We old folks are distasteful to the young).

Cf. Tilley, *Prov. in Eng.*, Y43.

BOOKS FREQUENTLY CITED

BOOKS FREQUENTLY CITED

With Explanation of Cue Titles

Anders, H. R. D. *Shakespeare's Books: A Dissertation on Shakespeare's Reading and the Immediate Sources of His Works* (Schriften der Deutschen Shakespeare-Gesellschaft, Band I). Berlin: Georg Reimer, 1904.

Bacon, Francis. *Promus of Formularies and Elegancies.* Illustrated and elucidated by passages from Shakespeare by Mrs. Henry Pott. London: Longmans, Green, and Co., 1883. Example of cue title with sample reference no.: Bacon, *Promus,* 357.

Baldwin, Thomas W. *William Shakspere's Small Latine & Lesse Greeke.* 2 vols. Urbana: University of Illinois Press, 1944.

Cato, Dionysius. *Dicta Catonis.* Edited and translated by J. Wight Duff and Arnold M. Duff and included in their *Minor Latin Poets.* Loeb Classical Library. Cambridge, Mass.: Harvard University Press, 1934. *Collectio Distichorum Vulgaris,* pp. 592–596. *Catonis Disticha,* pp. 596–621. *Collectio Monostichorum,* pp. 624–629.

Culman, Leonard [Leonhardus Culmannus]. *Sententiae Pueriles, Anglo-Latinae.* Translated by Charles Hoole. Londini: Sumptibus Societatis Stationariorum, 1658. Example of cue title with sample page no.: Culman, 10.

Erasmus, Desiderius. *Opera Omnia.* 10 vols. in 11. Leyden, 1703–1706. Vol. I: *Epistolas, Similia,* and *Colloquia Familiaria.* Vol. II: *Adagia.* Vol. IV: *Moriae Encomium.* Vol. V: *Enchiridion.* Example of cue title with sample page no.: Erasmus, *Similia,* 588C. *Institutio Principis Christiani,* 591C.

Shakespeare, William. *Complete Works.* Edited by George Lyman Kittredge. Boston: Ginn and Company, 1936.

Smith, William George. *Oxford Dictionary of English Proverbs.* With an Introduction by Janet E. Heseltine. Second edition, revised by Paul Harvey. Oxford: Clarendon Press, 1948. Example of cue title with sample page no.: Smith, 227.

Stevenson, Burton. *Home Book of Proverbs, Maxims and Familiar Phrases.*

New York: Macmillan Co., 1948. Example of cue title with sample page and reference no.: Stevenson, 516:2.

Syrus, Publilius. *Publilii Syri Sententiae*. Edited by R. A. H. Bickford-Smith. London: C. J. Clay and Sons, 1895.

—— *Sentences de Publius Syrus*. Traduction nouvelle par Jules Chenu. Paris: C. L. F. Panckoucke, 1835. Example of cue title with sample no. of a *sententia*: Publilius Syrus (1835), 229.

—— *Sententiae*. Edited and translated by J. Wight Duff and Arnold M. Duff and included in their *Minor Latin Poets*. Loeb Classical Library. Cambridge, Mass.: Harvard University Press, 1934. Example of cue title with sample no. of a *sententia*: Publilius Syrus (1934), 667.

Taverner, Richard. *Proverbs or Adages by Desiderius Erasmus*. Gathered out of the *Chiliades* and Englished by Richard Taverner, London, 1569. A facsimile reproduction with an Introduction by Dewitt T. Starnes. Gainsville, Florida: Scholar's Facsimiles & Reprints, 1956. Example of cue title with sample page no.: Taverner, 35.

Tilley, Morris Palmer. *Elizabethan Proverb Lore in Lyly's "Euphues" and in Pettie's "Petite Pallace."* New York: Macmillan Co., 1926. Example of cue title with the no. of a proverb: Tilley, *Eliz. Prov. Lore*, 52.

—— *A Dictionary of the Proverbs in England in the Sixteenth and Seventeenth Centuries*. Ann Arbor: University of Michigan Press, 1950. Example of cue title with the no. of a proverb: Tilley, *Prov. in Eng.*, F693.

Udall, Nicholas. *Apophthegmes of Erasmus*. Edited and illustrated with notes and parallel passages by Robert Roberts. Boston, Lincolnshire: Robert Roberts, 1877. Example of cue title with sample page and reference no.: Udall, *Apoph. of Erasm.*, 23:52.

DISTRIBUTION INDEX TO THE PROVERB LORE QUOTED FROM SHAKESPEARE

DISTRIBUTION INDEX TO THE PROVERB LORE QUOTED FROM SHAKESPEARE

This distribution index lists Shakespeare's works in alphabetical order and shows under each title where the proverb lore quoted from Shakespeare occurs. The numbers in parentheses following the citations refer to the entry numbers in the "List of Proverbs."

ALL'S WELL THAT ENDS WELL

I, i, 74-75 (34); I, i, 76-77 (267); I, i, 214-217 (259); I, i, 231-232 (1); I, i, 237-238 (180); I, i, 239-241 (51); I, iii, 26-28 (26); II, i, 145-147 (107); II, ii, 60-61 (168); II, iii, 20 (56); II, iii, 150-151 (24); II, iii, 222 (10); II, iv, 22-23 (267); II, v, 53 (143); III, iv, 42 (277); IV, i, 19-20 (96); IV, ii, 21-22 (304); IV, iv, 35-36 (79); IV, v, 105-106 (261); V, i, 15-16 (319); V, iii, 19-20 (249); V, iii, 105-106 (167); V, iii, 336 (79).

ANTONY AND CLEOPATRA

I, i, 42-43 (112); I, ii, 133-134 (157); II, v, 58-59 (307); II, vi, 2-3 (340); III, vi, 52-53 (311); III, xiii, 31-32 (245); IV, i, 9-10 (9); IV, iv, 20-21 (77); IV, vi, 25 (207); IV, xiv, 120-121 (197); IV, xiv, 135-138 (119); V, ii, 48-49 (208).

AS YOU LIKE IT

I, ii, 81-83 (154); II, i, 2-3 (48); II, i, 51-52 (234); II, vii, 18-19 (117); II, vii, 63-69 (97); II, vii, 102-103 (165); II, vii, 163-165 (25); II, vii, 181 (110); III, ii, 69 (171); III, ii, 206-207 (63); III, v, 57 (167); IV, iii, 129-131 (147); V, i, 35-36 (331); V, iv, 60-61 (181); Epil., 4, (328).

COMEDY OF ERRORS

I, i, 2 (53); I, i, 31-32 (248); II, i, 15 (174); II, ii, 66 (298); II, ii, 101-102

(298); IV, i, 112-113 (194); IV, iii, 76 (329); IV, iv, 20-21 (4); IV, iv, 44-46 (78).

CORIOLANUS

I, vi, 71 (55); II, i, 75-76 (167); II, i, 192 (266); II, ii, 88-89 (312); II, ii, 116 (66); II, iii, 124-126 (48); III, i, 152-153 (182); III, i, 218 (14); III, i, 258 (275); III, ii, 46-47 (14); III, iii, 88-89 (88); IV, i, 3-5 (20); IV, i, 6-7 (262); IV, vii, 11-12 (7); IV, vii, 37-39 (241); V, i, 18-19 (147); V, iii, 141 (321); V, iii, 154-155 (345).

CYMBELINE

I, i, 131-137 (264); I, i, 134-135 (8); I, iv, 146 (102); II, ii, 31 (271); II, iii, 47-49 (294); II, iii, 72-78 (209); II, iv, 143 (282); II, v, 30 (337); III, ii, 33 (5); III, iii, 79 (213); III, iv, 35-36 (270); III, iv, 157-158 (222); III, v, 37-38 (289); III, vi, 9 19 (226); IV, ii, 110 111 (197); IV, ii, 111-112 (163); IV, ii, 252-253 (54); V, iii, 57 (25); V, v, 75-76 (321); V, v, 417-419 (147).

HAMLET

I, i, 56-58 (90); I, ii, 72 (52, 67); I, ii, 146 (337); I, ii, 159 (227); I, iii, 38 (269); I, iii, 43 (259); I, iii, 47-51 (236); I, iii, 62-63 (306); I, iii, 68-69 (161); I, iv, 30-32 (211); I, iv, 30-38 (61); I, v, 43-45 (334); I, v, 43-45 (135); I, v, 128-131 (19); I, v, 188 (108); II, ii 403 (25);

II, ii, 571 (207); III, i, 78–82 (198); III, i, 100–101 (133); III, i, 107–108 (316); III, i, 140–141 (24); III, i, 140–142 (269); III, i, 158–161 (242); III, ii, 6–9 (208); III, ii, 177–178 (336); III, ii, 196 (275); III, ii, 202–203 (224); III, ii, 208–209 (160); III, ii, 210–211 (127); III, ii, 217 (252); III, ii, 218–219 (2); III, ii, 221–222 (120); III, iii, 41–43 (308); III, iv, 37–38 (49); III, iv, 161–162 (49); IV, iii, 4–7 (206); IV, iii, 9–11 (70); IV, iii, 24–26 (54); IV, iv, 39–44 (75); IV, v, 78–79 (204); IV, vi, 20–22 (307); IV, vii, 112–114 (294); IV, vii, 118–119 (255); IV, vii, 135–140 (286); IV, vii, 165 (204); IV, vii, 189 (213); V, i, 76 (48); V, i, 285–286 (102); V, ii, 10–11 (120); V, ii, 146–147 (167); V, ii, 189–192 (217); V, ii, 221–222 (235); V, ii, 222–224 (197).

1 HENRY IV

I, i, 105–107 (219); I, ii, 116–117 (320); I, iii, 94–95 (321); II, ii, 81 (19); II, iii, 111–112 (337); II, iv, 470–471 (301); III, ii, 57–59 (246); III, ii, 61–62 (335); III, ii, 71–72 (281); V, i, 120 (139); V, ii, 82 (179); V, iv, 139–140 (90); V, iv, 140 (14).

2 HENRY IV

I, i, 161–162 (219); I, i, 166–168 (321); I, iii, 108 (65); II, ii, 50–51 (79); II, ii, 80–83 (17); II, ii, 110–113 (150); II, iv, 303–304 (78); III, i, 88–90 (16); III, ii, 41–42 (56); III, ii, 42 (67); III, ii, 45 (56); IV, i, 196 (315); V, i, 72–76 (31); Epil., 21–22 (37).

HENRY V

I, ii, 172 (22); II, ii, 37 (251); II, ii, 54–57 (99); II, ii, 165 (273); II, iii, 52–53 (302); II, iv, 69–71 (72); III, vi, 29 (116); III, vi, 178 (138); III, vii, 124–125 (110); IV, i, 1–2 (41); IV, i, 4–5 (84); IV, v, 23 (55); V, ii, 402 (221).

1 HENRY VI

I, i, 75 (111); I, iv, 31–33 (55); II, i, 58–59 (322); II, iv, 20–21 (303); II, v,
28–29 (53); III, i, 72–73 (69); III, ii, 136 (67); III, ii, 136–137 (53); IV, iii, 43–44 (309); IV, iii, 49 (216); IV, v, 32–33 (55); IV, v, 40 (154); V, iii, 134 (116); V, iii, 141 (275); V, iv, 144–146 (43); V, v, 62 (188).

2 HENRY VI

I, i, 156–157 (334); I, i, 157 (329); I, iii, 155–157 (219); II, i, 19–20 (300); II, iii, 104 (178); III, i, 170–171 (71); III, i, 247 (275); III, i, 347 (324); III, iii, 5–6 (178); III, iii, 30 (178); III, iii, 31 (268); IV, ii, 17–18 (320); IV, ii, 184–185 (91); IV, iv, 55 (139); IV, iv, 58 (302); IV, x, 22 (132); V, i, 139–140 (91); V, i, 191 (13); V, ii, 28 (79).

3 HENRY VI

II, i, 54–55 (280); II, i, 85 (144); II, i, 96–99 (341); II, ii, 45–46 (86); II, vi, 22 (172); III, i, 24–25 (3); III, i, 90 (221); III, iii, 76–77 (289); IV, iii, 58 (66); IV, iv, 30 (16); IV, vi, 19–20 (118); IV, viii, 7–8 (274); V, i, 49 (279); V, ii, 28 (67); V, iv, 1 (330); V, iv, 37–38 (105); V, vi, 3 (109); V, vi, 11 (101); V, vi, 26–28 (341).

HENRY VIII

I, i, 16–17 (299); I, i, 123–125 (208); I, i, 160–161 (200); II, i, 127–130 (234); II, ii, 23 (167); II, iv, 17–18 (129); II, iv, 138–139 (222); III, i, 39 (305); III, i, 100–101 (137); III, i, 168–169 (318); IV, ii, 41–42 (243); IV, ii, 142–143 (176); V, i, 175–176 (279).

JULIUS CAESAR

I, ii, 139 (11); I, ii, 140–141 (1); I, ii, 194–209 (81); I, iii, 66–67 (23); II, i, 78–79 (218); II, i, 114 (282); II, ii, 26–27 (66); II, ii, 36–37 (56); III, i, 99 (56); III, ii, 81 (82); IV, i, 21–27 (12); IV, ii, 8–9 (74); IV, ii, 20–21 (42); IV, ii, 86 (123); IV, iii, 190–192 (67); V, i, 23–27 (340); V, i, 104–107 (120); V, iii, 40 (221).

OTHELLO

I, iii, 204–205 (248); I, iii, 206–207 (4);
I, iii, 230 (50); I, iii, 230–232 (48); I, iii,
290–291 (316); I, iii, 293–294 (16); I, iii,
301 (297); I, iii, 309–310 (58); I, iii,
322–323 (11); I, iii, 377–378 (287); I,
iii, 405–408 (286); II, i, 187 (278); II, i,
223–224 (108); II, iii, 105–107 (137); II,
iii, 206–207 (230); II, iii, 241 (333); II,
iii, 262–265 (44); II, iii, 376 (231); II,
iii, 385 (291); III, iii, 126–128 (14); III,
iii, 157–161 (94); III, iii, 172 (323);
III, iii, 342–343 (184); III, iii, 432 (329);
IV, ii, 184–185 (243); V, ii, 223 (329).

PASSIONATE PILGRIM

12, 1 (346); 17, 15 (116); 18, 5 (39); 20,
29 (115; 116); 20, 34 (126); 20, 35–36
(252); 20, 47–50 (121); 20, 51–52 (2).

PERICLES

I, Prol., 29–30 (49); I, i, 137 (83); I, ii, 39
(109); I, ii, 78 (106); I, iv, 63–64 (204);
I, iv, 75 (42); II, ii, 27 (165); II, iii, 12
(120); II, iv, 57–58 (310); II, v, 59 (60);
IV, ii, 131–132 (29); IV, iii, 1–6 (74);
IV, iii, 3–4 (25).

RICHARD II

I, i, 114 (175); I, i, 177–178 (94); I, i,
182–183 (44); I, ii, 6–8 (313); I, iii,
154–155 (85); I, iii, 182 (221); I, iii,
260–261 (291); I, iii, 261 (177); I, iii,
275–276 (332); I, iii, 280–281 (159); I,
iii, 292–293 (159); II, i, 91–93 (150);
II, i, 152 (53); II, i, 266 (263); III, ii,
29–30 (140); III, ii, 103 (56); III, ii,
178 (330); III, ii, 193 (166); III, iii, 17–
19 (137); III, iv, 2 (21); III, iv, 28
(204); IV, i, 317–318 (256); V, i, 90
(183); V, iii, 64 (255).

RICHARD III

I, ii, 68–69 (143); I, iii, 183–184 (164);
I, iii, 222 (36); I, iii, 259–260 (152); I,
iii, 289–290 (42); I, iii, 335 (143); II, iii,
42–43 (197); III, i, 79 (335); IV, i, 79–80
(342); IV, ii, 34–35 (141); IV, ii, 38

(142); IV, iv, 82–90 (191); IV, iv, 116–
119 (203); IV, iv, 126–131 (277); IV, iv,
218 (66); IV, iv, 291 (74); IV, iv, 292–
293 (205); IV, iv, 358 (303); IV, iv, 395
(282); IV, iv, 431 (337); V, ii, 17–18
(35); V, iii, 73–74 (197); V, iii, 194–196
(35).

ROMEO AND JULIET

I, i, 168 (177); I, i, 186–189 (185); I, i,
221 (141); I, ii, 104–105 (181); I, iv,
106–107 (197); II, Prol., 13–14 (70); II,
ii, 92–93 (220); II, ii, 109 (282); II, ii,
112 (282); II, ii, 116 (282); II, iii, 36
(272); II, iii, 93–94 (148); II, iv, 155–157
(243); II, vi, 15 (149); III, i, 202 (172);
III, ii, 89 (45); III, ii, 116 (30); III, iii,
13–14 (88); III, iii, 43 (88); III, iii, 92
(67); III, iv, 4 (67); III, v, 52–53 (249);
III, v, 60 (116); IV, i, 68–70 (70); IV, v,
90 (23); V, i, 35–36 (200); V, i, 80–82
(141); V, iii, 153–154 (120); V, iii, 212
(45); V, iii, 294–295 (99).

SONNETS

19, 1 (290); 19, 6 (292); 20, 4 (337); 24, 9
(307); 35, 5 (98); 47, 2 (307); 52, 2–7
(246); 94, 1–5 (147); 102, 12 (95); 116,
1–2 (199); 116, 2–3 (131); 119, 9–10
(84); 119, 11–12 (92); 152, 5–6 (97).

TAMING OF THE SHREW

IV, ii, 36 (221); V, i, 155 (169).

TEMPEST

I, ii, 97–103 (173); I, ii, 304 (68); I, ii,
450–452 (240); I, ii, 496–497 (214); II, i,
16–19 (202); III, i, 29–31 (327); III, i,
53–54 (24); IV, i, 53 (208); IV, i, 188–
189 (212); V, i, 27–28 (147); V, i, 123
(282); V, i, 199–200 (248); V, i, 256–258
(120).

TIMON OF ATHENS

I, i, 15–17 (153); I, i, 170–171 (181); I, i,
288–291 (134); I, ii, 10–11 (136); I, ii,
15–18 (42); I, ii, 63–67 (338); I, ii, 64–66
(302); I, ii, 98–101 (128); I, ii, 105 (18);

LATIN AND ENGLISH WORD INDEXES

LATIN WORD INDEX

This index contains the main words in all the *sententiae* quoted. The numbers refer to the entry numbers in the "List of Proverbs."

bonos, 86, 169
bonum, 10, 106, 182, 254, 317
bonus, 14, 124, 175, 187
brevis, 177, 179, 291
bulla, 191
bullae, 191

caecitatem, 230
caedere, 71
caelo, 167
calamitas, 2, 183, 204, 248, 250
calamitate, 250
calamitatem, 248, 263
calamitati, 40
calamitatum, 30
calcar, 93
candet, 279
canem, 71, 72
canes, 72
capit, 308
capiunt, 135
captat, 308
caput, 158
caret, 322
carminibus, 11
carum, 246
carus, 187
casta, 222
casu, 30
casus, 152
causa, 162
causam, 161
cave, 14, 16, 306
cavendum, 16
cavendus, 170
cavet, 322
cedere, 40
celare, 20
celat, 214
celerius, 335
celerrime, 292
cernere, 97, 230
cernitur, 2
certat, 185
certe, 67
certissima, 29
certius, 56
certus, 2
cibi, 156

cicatrix, 261, 343
citius, 216
cito, 116, 326, 335
clementia, 29
cluet, 126
coepit, 131
coetui, 346
cogit, 194, 226
cogitant, 313
cogitat, 144, 202, 275
cognatio, 199
cognitam, 161
cognosce, 167
cognoscimus, 2
cognoscit, 73
cognoscitur, 2, 214, 301
cognosco, 301
cognoscuntur, 2
coguntur, 70
color, 17
comes, 148, 257
comi, 122
comibus, 186
comitari, 137
comites, 148
commendat, 246
comminuit, 117
committitur, 324
commodum, 308
commune, 65, 125, 205, 265
communia, 125
communis, 52
comparat, 29
comparatio, 32
compatiens, 30
compendiariam, 14
compesce, 108
compescere, 258
concedas, 134
conceditur, 190
conciliant, 186, 252
concordia, 310
condimentum, 156, 338
condit, 156
condiuntur, 233
confessio, 33
confidendum, 302
confingunt, 11
confinia, 315

ENGLISH WORD INDEX

This is a catchword index to the proverb lore quoted from Shakespeare and to the translations of all the *sententiae* quoted. The numbers refer to the entry numbers in the "List of Proverbs."

God, 5, 26, 89, 120, 137, 138, 139, 140, 313
gold, 12, 141, 142, 209
good, 5, 30, 37, 84, 106, 143, 175, 239, 255, 293, 307, 309, 314, 315, 328
goodness, 84, 255
goods, 86, 125
govern, 120
grace, 5, 264, 266
gratify, 285
gravelled, 75
graze, 12
great, 41, 243, 274
greater, 152, 183, 240
greatest, 323
greed, 210
grief, 30, 144, 160, 177, 227, 248, 277, 291, 296
griefs, 5, 45
grievous, 85
groan, 12
grows, 81
grumble, 1
guilt, 178
guilty, 97, 101, 145, 229

hammer, 279
hand, 138, 324
hang, 328
happiness, 203
happy, 256, 263, 291
hard, 61, 126, 240
hares, 146, 308
harm, 8, 102, 147, 267, 286, 314, 344
harmful, 276, 284
haste, 148, 149
hasten, 45
hate, 175, 336
haughtiness, 241
hazards, 41
healed, 343
heals, 289
health, 150
hear, 90, 161
heart, 189, 227, 275, 300
heaven, 1, 137, 313
hell, 227
helm, 262
help, 2, 7, 89, 139, 140, 309

hesitant, 151
hidden, 122
higher, 152
highest, 62
himself, 18, 140, 217
hold, 254
honest, 60, 239
honey, 185
honor, 44, 55, 93, 153, 154, 261, 276
honorable, 55, 215
hope, 155, 251, 264
hot, 279
hour, 291
human, 120
hunger, 156, 260
hurt, 38, 145, 187, 284
husband, 222

idleness, 157
ignorance, 225
ill, 31, 103, 119, 178
ill-doing, 326
ill-gotten, 86
ills, 1, 5, 20, 177, 183, 249, 289
ill-spent, 86
image, 271
impose, 66
impossible, 190
impotent, 142
impute, 1
inconstant, 337
increase, 51, 228
incur, 51
indulges, 9
industrious, 140
infamy, 55, 61
infirmity, 123
inflict, 8
ingratitude, 158
iniquity, 229
injure, 8, 145
injuries, 159
injurious, 270
injury, 225
innocence, 33
innocent, 145, 226
instruction, 236
instructor, 13
invincible, 209